FLY FISHING THE TEXAS COAST
BACKCOUNTRY FLATS TO BLUEWATER

FLY FISHING THE TEXAS COAST
BACKCOUNTRY FLATS TO BLUEWATER

CHUCK SCATES AND PHIL H. SHOOK

PHOTOGRAPHS BY DAVID J. SAMS

MAPS BY ROBERT DIBRELL

PRUETT PUBLISHING COMPANY
BOULDER, COLORADO

Printed in the United States

08 07 06 05 04 03 02 01 00   5 4 3

Library of Congress Cataloging-in-Publication Data

Scates, Chuck, 1954–
    Fly fishing the Texas coast : backcountry flats to bluewater /
Chuck Scates and Phil H. Shook ; photography by David J. Sams ; maps
by Robert Dibrell.
        p.   cm.
    Includes bibliographical references (p.   ) and index.
    ISBN 0-87108-888-6 (pbk.)
    1. Saltwater fly fishing—Texas. I. Shook, Phil, 1942–   .
II. Title.
SH551.S28   1999
799.1'6'09764—dc21   99-27350
                                                                CIP

Cover and book design by Michael Signorella, Studio Signorella
Book composition by Lyn Chaffee
Cover and interior photographs by David J. Sams
Maps by Robert Dibrell

To the flyfishers of Texas
—CS

To Janet and Phil, shrimp boats in watercolors,
and those long summer days at Studeman's
—PHS

To the fish; find 'em, catch 'em, release 'em
—DJS

CONTENTS

FOREWORD

After years of conducting fly fishing seminars around the world, I still find Texan hospitality very special. So every year I make it my business to fish some area of Texas. But because Texas has so much fishable terrain, I am always asking some local expert or writer where to go. I know I have burned Chuck Scates's ear off with such questions over the years.

Maybe now I won't need to bother Chuck or other Texas friends so often. This wonderful book describes where, when, and how to fly fish the Texas Coast.

And the recipe for the book is ideal.

All three of the book's collaborators have been around Texas waters most of their lives, picking up fly fishing as most of us saltwater devotees have done. I am of the opinion that the best background flyfishers can bring to the sport includes experience with all or most other types of fishing: bait, live bait, casting lures, etc., experience that they can apply to fly fishing. The three anglers who have produced this book bring all of this and more to the reader. Veteran angler Chuck Scates, one of the first fly-fishing guides in Texas, provides information from the eyes of a guide; David J. Sams, a flyfisher and award-winning photographer, provides images taken from an angler's point of view. And Phil Shook, a skilled, twenty-year veteran of the sport himself, provides insights from his many years of research and writing on saltwater fly fishing.

The book covers the whole Texas coastline, from its bays, beaches, and flats to its offshore waters. It includes detailed information on every kind of coastal terrain and on a variety of possible fishing conditions: climate and seasonal changes, necessary skills and techniques, the best tackle and gear, day and night fishing, and so on. My particular fascination with the Texas surf (all 367 miles of it) receives healthy coverage here and, as with all other aspects of the book, the authors draw not only from their own experience but from that of numerous experts in the field for accurate information. I literally read this section of the book twice.

Most people skim a book before writing a foreword. I started to do that with this book but ended up reading the entire manuscript. And I fully intend to read it again. The book carries a balanced conservation message, presented logically and without extremes, that I fully support; I am proud of the authors for including it. The accurate, honest information presented in this book is a must for anyone wanting to fly fish in Texas. I can't envision an angler planning a trip to the Texas coast without carrying this book under his or her arm.

—J. M. Chico Fernandez
December 1998

PREFACE

Redfish Lodge on Copano Bay
Rockport, Texas
October 1998

With this book, we invite readers on a Texas coastal fly-fishing adventure. Travel with us from the bayou country near the Louisiana border to the mangrove-lined estuaries and grass flats of the Lower Laguna Madre near the Mexican border. From the experiences of veteran flyfishers, guides, and outfitters, we have selected the best ways to fly fish the surf along the longest barrier island in the world, and together we will try them out: We will wade the warm waters of the Laguna Madre, along the shoreline of the storied King Ranch, and cast our lines in Baffin Bay, Texas's big trout haven. We will seek adventure, too, around the arroyos and estuaries near the Rio Grande, where flyfishers are challenged to land snook, speckled trout, redfish, and tarpon—the Texas angler's grand slam.

Our goal is to help anglers have a memorable experience in fly fishing the Texas coast. We have made an effort to provide practical information in a format that is accessible to all flyfishers—beginners and veterans alike—who are eager to string up their rods and begin fishing. We address the technical requirements of saltwater fly fishing within each chapter and make suggestions on suitable tackle and techniques in the context of each destination and fishing situation.

Although the three of us are committed saltwater flyfishers with decades of experience fishing Texas's coastal waters, we cannot claim to know every flat, backcountry lake, channel, beachfront, jetty rock, or blue water platform where fish will take a well-presented fly. We are constantly discovering new fly-fishing opportunities every time we leave a launch ramp or travel along the coast. Therefore, we have called on and received the gracious assistance of some of Texas's most experienced flyfishers, including veteran guides, the International Game Fish Association (IGFA) world record holders, outfitters, bluewater captains, shrimp boat operators, marine weather forecasters, fisheries biologists, fly shop proprietors, and longtime anglers.

Like most Texas anglers, we started out fishing from piers and wharfs with cane poles and dead bait. We've fished with live shrimp under popping corks, thrown surf rods, used spinning tackle, and pitched Mirr-O-Lures and gold spoons. Along the way, with the development and refinement of specialized fly lines, composite graphite rods, and high-capacity, disc-drag saltwater reels, we discovered coastal fly fishing and rediscovered fishing. We found that it was a natural for our saltwater flats as well as our fresh-water lakes and ponds. In the process, we learned how effective the flyrod can be and how this form of angling is so naturally suited to our magnificent coastal environment. For us, fly fishing has brought new levels of adventure to saltwater angling and helped us rediscover our shores. We hope this guide helps others to discover the adventure of fly fishing the Texas coast.

David J. Sams
Chuck Scates
Phil H. Shook

ACKNOWLEDGMENTS

A host of flyfishers, fly tyers, guides, outfitters, sea captains, innkeepers, and raconteurs have been generous in sharing with us their time, talents, resources, and insight. Without their support, this book would not have been possible.

We would like to recognize the following people for their help: Barry Austin, Capt. Dana Bailey, Terry Baird, Mike Barbee, Capt. Thomas Barnard, Kenneth Bay, Brooks Bouldin, Barry Box, Ray Box, Larry Bozka, Jon Bradford, Ken Brumbaugh, Frank Budd, Sam Caldwell, Kenneth O. Callaway, Sr., Raymond Chapa, Capt. Dan Coley, Bob Colura, Jim Cox, Capt. Robert Crumpler, Charlie Cypert, Jim Dailey, Dr. Scott Daniel, Kevin Daniels, Tim Debord, Joe DeForke, Henk DeWitt, James Doggett, Joe Doggett, Malcolm Duke, Charles Dukes, Wade Duncan, Charles Duvic, Dan Edwards, Capt. Gary Einkauf, Marcos Enriquez, Capt. Jon Fails, Capt. Shawn Flanagan, Rick Fleming, Capt. Jim Foster, Capt. James Fox, Dennis Freeman, Capt. Jim Friebele, Capt. Charlie Fulghum, Capt. Smokey Gaines, Capt. Bob Gardner, O. C. Garza, Ken Geiger, Bruce Gillan, Sherry Gillan, Capt. Eric Glass, Buddy Gough, Capt. Dan Goyen, Rob Gregoire, Anthony Grice, Capt. Don Hand, Tom Hargrave, Dave Hayward, Layton Hobbs, Larry Hoffman, Capt. Brian Holden, Jack Holder, Capt. Matt Hoover, Capt. Frank Houser, Mike Huffman, Capt. Skip James, Jeff Johnson, Capt. Russ Jones, Tom Kasey, Dede Kasey, Bill Kenner, Capt. Mark Klotzman, Spencer Klotzman, Capt. Mark Koliba, Brad Kottinger, Jim Kuper, Richard Laird, Capt. Jim Leavelle, Mike Leggett, Les Lehman, Lee Leschper, Neal Lillard, Capt. Gib Little, Jerry Loring, Capt. Dwayne Lowery, Mark Lucas, Dan Lynch, Capt. Fred Lynch, Jeff McDowell, Larry McEachron, Richard McInnis, Charly McTee, Tony Maessen, W. B. "Sonny" Mahan, Cary Marcus, Thom Marshall, Capt. Walter Mayer, Ron Mayfield, Alex Mehl, Capt. John Mendleski, Bob Miller, Bill Minor, Allan Ray Moers, Kenneth J. Murph, Capt. Chuck Naiser, Capt. Terry Neal, T. J. Neal, William Negley, Capt. Jack Nelson, Capt. Lowell Odom, Jim Olive, Tira Overstreet, Andy Packmore, Capt. Chris Phillips, Doug Pike, Capt. James Plaag, Capt. Cory Rich, Ronnie Robison, Billy Sandifer, Ray Sasser, Capt. Bill Schneider, Ryan Seiders, Lindsay Sharpe, Reggie Sheffield, Capt. Bill Sheka, Lt. Cdr. Eric Shirey, Capt. Darrell Skillern, Capt. Bill Smith, Capt. Brad Smythe, Capt. Scott Sommerlatte, Barkley Souders, Capt. Jim Stewart, Bill Stoneberg, Capt. Mike Sydow, Russell Tinsley,

Shannon Tompkins, Capt. James Trimble, William Trout, Capt. Chuck Uzzle, Dr. Gonzalo Vargas, Robert Vega, Capt. Gilbert Vela, John Warren, Todd Winn, Capt. Sam Wigginton, Ross Wilhite, Capt. Mike Williams, Todd Woodard, Reavis Wortham, and Art Wright.

Our special thanks go to Jerry Moulden of Shoreline Publishing and Kent Simons with Haywood Graphics for their assistance in producing maps and graphics. We are grateful to Nick Lyons for his generous advice and encouragement, to Jeffrey Hines for his good counsel, and we are indebted to Robert Dibrell for his mapmaking skills. Our gratitude also goes to Marykay Scott and Kim Adams, our editors, and Craig Martin for their advice and perspective in shaping this book.

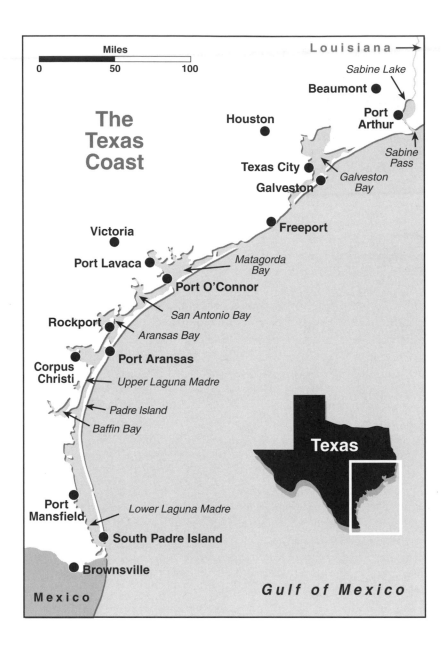

Miles
0   50   100

The
Texas
Coast

Louisiana →

Sabine Lake

Beaumont ●

Houston ●

Port
Arthur ●

Sabine
Pass

Texas City ●

Galveston ●

Galveston
Bay

Victoria ●

Freeport ●

Port Lavaca ●

Matagorda
Bay

Port O'Connor ●

San Antonio Bay

Rockport ●

Aransas Bay

Port Aransas ●

Corpus
Christi ●

Upper Laguna Madre

Padre Island

Baffin Bay

Texas

Port
Mansfield ●

Lower Laguna Madre

South Padre Island ●

Brownsville ●

Mexico

Gulf of Mexico

CHAPTER ONE

THE TEXAS GULF COAST

A FLY-FISHING FRONTIER

From shorelines silhouetted in cactus and mesquite to clear-water estuaries where whooping cranes wade among tailing redfish, the Texas Coast offers unique and diverse locales for saltwater fly fishing. ❧ Casting from the bow of a johnboat as it is poled along Madame Johnson Bayou on Sabine Lake, a large bay system that forms a border between Texas and Louisiana, flyfishers draw strikes from southern flounder that cannot resist a mud minnow fly imitation. On the trip you might see scruffy feral hogs wandering along thick stands of rosso cane near the water's edge. Alligators, too, are often spotted scurrying off the bank at the approach of a boat.

To get to this fishery, flyfishers and guides launch from an old-fashioned marina with a rickety pier and motor under cypress and oak trees draped in moss and past refinery loading docks and inviting shorelines with shell bars and tidal creeks before reaching the opening to Sabine Lake. A half-hour ride across the lake's early morning chop brings them to the remote bayous of the Sabine National Wildlife Refuge, in search of the schools of speckled trout that feed around the creek mouths and oyster bars and the redfish that leave V-shaped wakes in the still water.

About 70 nautical miles south of Madame Johnson Bayou, on the other side of a pass from Galveston's bustling summer beach crowd, flyfishers can enjoy a totally different environment. Using 10-weight fly rods and fishing from boats, they launch shooting taper lines toward marauding bands of "bull reds" hazing an acre-wide school of menhaden just off the Bolivar Peninsula surfline.

Two hundred miles south of Galveston, flyfishers depart from the launch ramp at Goose Island State Park for exciting backcountry fishing north of Rockport. The trip includes frequent sightings of egrets, roseate spoonbills, and ibises wading through lagoons on the Blackjack Peninsula. In the fall and winter months, whooping cranes are seen along the grasslands and marshes of the Aransas National Wildlife Refuge. The backcountry

Guide poles flyfisher on flats near Rockport.

Angler Reavis Wortham with southern flounder, caught on Clouser Deep Minnow.

Endangered whooping cranes fish for crabs at their fall and winter home on the Aransas National Wildlife Refuge.

lakes behind Matagorda and San Jose islands also offer sightcasting to tailing redfish in water barely above the ankles.

Farther south, in nearshore Gulf waters off Padre Island near the Mexican border, flyfishers scan the surfline behind Polaroid lenses, searching the horizon for diving birds or baitfish being kicked up on the surface. They look for schools of cruising tarpon near the mouth of the Rio Grande, an ancestral home of the silver king.

With the growing interest in saltwater fly fishing, the Texas coast has emerged as an exciting frontier where new adventures are being discovered by flyfishers every day on backcountry lakes and barrier island beaches and around offshore oil platforms and reefs.

BARRIER ISLANDS, BACK BAYS, AND BEACHFRONTS

The 367-mile Texas coast, the third longest coastline among the states, lies on a large, flat plain. Principal ports on the Gulf are Galveston, Corpus Christi, and Brownsville, and Houston is the primary inland port. Along the Gulf of Mexico shoreline, a string of long, narrow barrier islands and peninsulas parallels the mainland. Behind these islands and peninsulas is a series of estuaries—long, shallow embayments at the mouths of large rivers. These bays are rimmed by shallow lagoons commonly called "flats." Accessible to shallow-draft boats and popular with wadefishers, these flats contain sand and mud bottoms, grass beds, oyster reefs, brackish ponds, and tidal creeks—and an abundance of gamefish and shellfish.

Eight large estuaries that receive freshwater inflows from Texas rivers lie along the coast from the Louisiana border to the Rio Grande: the Sabine-Neches and Trinity–San Jacinto estuaries are located on the upper coast; the East Matagorda, Lavaca–Tres Palacios, Guadalupe, Mission-Aransas, and Nueces, on the middle coast; and the Laguna Madre, on the lower coast. The estuaries are a vital link in the complex marine ecosystem. Texas Parks and Wildlife Department studies have shown that virtually all of the fish and shellfish taken by commercial and recreational fishermen in Texas depend on estuaries for at least a portion of their life cycles. The marshlands found between the estuaries and uplands also are vital to the estuarine ecosystem, providing nurseries for red drum, spotted seatrout, and shrimp. The regulation of salinity levels is a critical function of freshwater inflows, enabling the survival of many organisms that cannot live either in fresh water or in water with the salinity level of the open Gulf.

CLIMATE, SEASONS, AND STORMS

The average seasonal temperature of the Texas coast rivals that of Florida, and sea breezes make even hot summers pleasant: The average reading in the spring is 73.2 degrees; in the summer, 82.8; fall, 77.4; and winter, 65.5, according to the annually published *Texas Almanac*.

Two traditional and recognizable weather patterns common to the Texas coast are steady onshore breezes in the summer and northers in winter. These patterns affect access to fishing, water clarity, and water levels in bays, among other things. The prevailing southeasterlies that sweep across the barrier islands between March and November generate the northeast-by-southwest wave patterns that wash across the Gulf side. The smaller, shallower bay systems of the middle and lower coasts receive a measure of protection from the barrier islands. Anglers can often find clear flats and lighter winds on the leeward side of these islands.

Roughly from mid-November through the end of February, polar air masses bellow down to the Gulf from the north. These northers, although usually no more than three days in duration, can generate wind velocities up to 40 or 50 miles per hour (mph), roiling the bays and pushing water from the mainland shore up against the barrier island shorelines. Boaters and anglers can find protected shorelines in stiff southeasterlies, but a "blue norther" muddies bay waters and shuts down virtually all boating and fishing activities.

4

Sea kayaking at sun up, Cavasso Creek.

Violent tropical depressions and full-blown hurricanes also wheel out of the Gulf of Mexico and slam into the Texas coast with regularity, especially during hurricane season, which officially begins June 1 and ends November 30. Among the worst in modern times were Carla, which took 34 lives in 1961, with winds that reached 175 mph; Beulah, which caused 13 deaths and $150 million in property losses in 1967; and Celia, which took 11 lives in 1970. Alicia killed 18 and injured 1,800 in 1983. Records indicate that some sort of tropical storm makes landfall along the Texas coast every three to four years and that such storms reach hurricane force every four to five years and earn the title of severe hurricanes once in a decade or so. Anglers fishing the bays and Gulf waters should be aware of weather conditions and forecasts at all times. Weather can be picture-perfect before a storm, and fishing can be excellent. The fishery is normally unaffected by these major storms, although coastal communities often need time to recover from the ravages of wind, storm surges, and flooding that can result from violent storms.

THE GAMEFISH OF THE TEXAS COAST

Besides an abundance of redfish and seatrout—the most popular inshore gamefish—flyfishers take a variety of other species in Texas bays and estuaries, including flounder, black drum, jack crevalle, ladyfish, and sheepshead. With today's large-capacity saltwater reels and specialized fly lines, new vistas have opened for saltwater fly fishing in Texas. Flyfishers now routinely take Spanish mackerel, small grouper, bluefish, little tunny (false albacore), blue runners, and amberjack around jetty rocks and nearshore oil platforms. And when favorable winds and currents bring clear, green water and swarms of baitfish and predator fish close to the beach, flyfishers wade out into the surf, often for day-long action with trout, redfish, pompano, Spanish mackerel, and ladyfish. In the offshore Gulf waters around Texas ports, flyfishers can hook ling (cobia), king mackerel, blackfin tuna, wahoo, and dolphin near weedlines, oil platforms, and anchored shrimp boats.

CHAPTER TWO

FLY FISHING THE TEXAS COAST

AN OVERVIEW

A REGION RICH IN HISTORY

Centuries before composite graphite fly rods, disc-drag reels, and weight-forward fly lines were invented, Karankawa Indians were fishing the bays, beaches, and estuaries of Texas. The Karankawa, who were called "Water Walkers" by early explorers and settlers in the area, lived in a harsh environment and were known to smear alligator fat on their bodies to ward off biting insects. Perhaps because of this, they were generally considered by whites to be a foul-smelling and ill-tempered people. Catch-and-release was not practiced by the Karankawa either with gamefish or with Spanish explorers.

Whereas the Karankawa presence dates back to the fourteenth century, the first European known to have set foot on a Texas shoreline was Spanish explorer Alonso Alvarez de Pineda, who on an expedition looking for a shortcut to India, landed his four ships on the southern tip of Texas in 1519. The first detailed description of the land now called Texas was penned by Alvar Núñez Cabeza de Vaca, treasurer on another Spanish expedition, in 1528. Shipwrecked near Galveston Island, de Vaca survived to chronicle his eight years among the Indians as a captive, trader, and medicine man.

In 1553 a fleet of ships departing for Spain from Veracruz, Mexico, laden with Aztec treasure and with a thousand conquistadors and their families, was caught in a hurricane and cast up on the shores of Padre Island. Thirteen ships made safe landing at Devil's Elbow, a stretch of beach that is now a part of the Padre Island National Seashore. On a desperate overland trek southward to Mexico, the survivors were set upon by Karankawa. Only two lived long enough to tell the story.

Storm victims were the most frequent visitors to the Texas coast in the ensuing years, until French explorer Rene Robert Cavelier, Sieur de la Salle, discoverer of the Mississippi, arrived at Matagorda Bay in 1685. La Salle's expedition built a fort and named the nearby bay La Vaca. The settlement suffered hardships, and La Salle would later be murdered by one of his men

Sand dunes along the edges of Padre Island.

near the Brazos River. When Spanish explorer Alonso de Leon arrived at the fort in 1689, he found only the remains of a few French colonists, who had fallen victim to the Karankawa.

De Leon's foray launched a period of competition between Spanish, French, and American colonists to settle Texas. In 1804 a Spanish mariner priest named Padre Nicolas Balli and his nephew, Juan Jose Balli, established a ranch about 25 miles north of what is now Port Isabel and South Padre Island. Padre Island, Texas's southernmost barrier island, is named for the pioneer priest. Meanwhile, from the early 1800s until about 1821, pirate Louis Aury and privateer Jean Lafitte traded slaves out of the port of Galveston and raided Spanish shipping from their Matagorda Island hideaways. Colonists from the United States began coming to Texas in the early nineteenth century and by 1836 they united in war to win independence from Mexico.

Vast stretches of the Texas coast, including the 69.5-mile Padre Island National Seashore, remain much as they were when the Karankawa, Spaniards, French, and pirates explored these shores. Several islands, including Matagorda, San Jose, and Padre Island National Seashore are virtually uninhabited. Some are privately owned and inaccessible, whereas others are managed as state parks and wildlife refuges and share the shoreline with high-rise resort complexes.

The Modern Angling Era

Although saltwater fly fishing has become popular relatively recently on the Texas flats, the Texas coast has a rich angling history. In the early 1900s, the region was already established as a world-class fishing ground. Noted anglers from all over the country who over the years came to fish for tarpon at Port Aransas, stayed at the Tarpon Inn, a resort hotel that is still open today. In 1906, guests staying at the Tarpon Inn could fish from skiffs tied together and towed out to the jetties by sailboat, for $3.50 a day. That year's Tarpon Inn proprietor, J. E. Cotter, reported that visiting anglers caught 1,537 tarpon during the April-to-November fishing season.

Over the years the great Texas tarpon fishery has attracted world-class anglers to Port Aransas, including Charles Frederick Holder, founder in 1898 of the Tuna Club of Avalon, Santa Catalina Island, California; Richard Sutton, author of *The Silver Kings of Aransas Pass*; and fabled angler and author S. Kip Farrington, Jr. Of the many notable angling events that have taken place in Texas, none is more celebrated than Franklin Delano Roosevelt's visit to the waters around Port Aransas in 1937 to sample the tarpon fishing. The president, looking like any summer tourist in floppy hat and long-sleeved shirt, fished with local guides and fought and landed tarpon on two trips to the nearby jetties.

The great migrations of tarpon that thrived in Texas waters began to decline in the mid-1960s. Although no scientific investigation has been conducted into the cause of this decline, a number of factors have been suggested, including the damming of rivers, which has led to restricted freshwater inflows to marine estuaries; the increased inshore boating activity; pollution by runoff of agricultural pesticides; netting and dynamiting of tarpon schools in the rivers of Mexico; and shifts in baitfish migration patterns.

In recent years, tarpon have returned to Texas's nearshore waters in good numbers. Despite several hard freezes, which wreaked havoc on fish stocks in Texas's shallow estuaries, fishing for inshore species has shown remarkable gains in quantity and quality in recent seasons. A decade-long effort by anglers, marine conservation groups, and state fisheries officials to conserve the resource, remove commercial netting from bay waters, reduce size and bag limits, and supplement gamefish stocks through a soundly managed marine hatchery program are paying off. Dockside creel surveys and bag seine sampling by Texas Parks and Wildlife Department officials back up the fish stories being told by anglers from Sabine Pass to Brownsville.

SAFETY HAZARDS AND PRECAUTIONS

Whether wading a flat, walking into the surf, or fishing from the deck of a boat, anglers face a number of hazards. All should be kept in mind when you are planning your coastal fishing expedition.

Protection from the Sun

The sun's rays, reflecting off of light sand bottoms and boat decks, probably inflict more pain on more people than any other single hazard on the Texas coast. Even on days with cool breezes or overcast skies, long-billed hats, sunglasses, and generous applications of sunscreen are musts. A sure way to avoid the harmful rays of the sun is to wear pants and a long-sleeved shirt. An ideal fabric is a mix of cotton and polyester or nylon. Many guides also recommend a hat with a lightweight mask that snaps under sunglasses, shielding the whole face from both sun and wind.

Although lightweight diver's booties are adequate for wading flats with hard, sand bottoms, old tennis shoes or wading boots with solid rubber soles offer much more protection around oyster bars and scattered shell.

Stingrays and Jellyfish

The Atlantic stingray, a brown-colored flatfish with eyes atop its head, is prevalent in Texas waters. Its active presence on flats and shorelines is disturbing to some anglers and welcomed by others. The appearance of rays often is a sign that gamefish are actively feeding in the area. If left alone, stingrays are docile fish; but they react defensively when stepped on, inflicting a nonfatal but extremely painful and serious wound with the serrated spine or barb at the base of their tail. To avoid a confrontation with a stingray, wadefishers develop the habit of sliding or shuffling their feet to warn any unseen ray to move out of the way. As an added protection, some anglers wear the lightweight, protective leggings sold at many tackle stores in Texas.

Pants and long-sleeved shirts are usually the best defense against the bothersome but relatively minor stings that can result from contact with the jellyfish common to Texas bays. Portuguese man-of-war, a community of marine organisms with long streamers extending from a neon purple-and-pink balloon-like bladder, inflict a more severe sting. They turn up most often on the Gulf side of the barrier islands, in the surf and around passes. They are easy to see as they float on the surface, and should be given a wide berth.

Dealing with Soft Bottoms on the Flats

When firm, sand bottoms suddenly become soft and boggy, waders should remain calm and back out slowly. If a wader sinks to upper calf level in mud, an effective approach is to get down on hands and knees and crawl out. In extremely soft mud that comes close to waist level—fortunately, an uncommon occurrence on the Texas flats—waders are advised to lie down, as flat as possible, and swim out.

RULES, REGULATIONS, AND CONSERVATION

Anglers must have a fishing license and saltwater stamp to fish Texas coastal waters. Resident and nonresident anglers seventeen years of age or older also must possess a driver's license or personal identification certificate when fishing Texas waters. Recreational fishing licenses are sold at sporting goods stores, bait and tackle shops, and grocery stores throughout the state. For information on size and bag limits for Texas saltwater species, contact the Texas Parks and Wildlife Department (TPWD) at 1-800-792-1112. For information on licenses and stamps, call 1-800-895-4248.

Conservation Practices

A conservation ethic based on the recognition that gamefish populations and the marine environments that support them are fragile and finite resources is a continuing tradition in Texas. In 1955 the Port Aransas Rod & Reel Club instituted a program of tagging and releasing gamefish, particularly tarpon and billfish, as a way to aid in research and promote conservation in sportfishing. In 1977, after several years of alarming declines in inshore fish populations, fourteen anglers gathered in a Houston sporting goods store to form the Gulf Coast Conservation Association (GCCA), which later expanded to other states to become the Coastal Conservation Association (CCA). They were concerned that bay fisheries could not withstand the onslaught from commercial netting. What started in Texas with the battle cry to "save the redfish" has now spread across the country with CCA chapters springing up everywhere from Texas to Florida and from Georgia to Maine.

Today redfish, speckled trout, and a dozen other marine species come under the protective influence of CCA–Texas. The angling and conservation group also focuses on a multitude of issues related to the protection of the coastal environment, from seagrass restoration to freshwater inflows. Through the state legislature, often in partnership with the Texas Parks and Wildlife Department, CCA–Texas serves as a watchdog over coastal issues. The organization is recognized as a model for other marine conservation programs by groups like the CCA and marine fisheries departments in other states.

Texas Marine Hatchery and Stocking Programs

An ambitious marine hatchery program designed to supplement and enhance existing gamefish stocks, along with a ban on commercial netting,

*Phil Shook sports a 25-inch red drum, caught from his
sea kayak near Aransas Bay.*

tighter size and bag limits, and a string of mild winters, is credited for the
resurgence in the spotted seatrout and red drum populations in Texas waters. A fishery that was struggling two decades ago and devastated by killer
freezes in 1983 and 1989 has rebounded in quality and quantity, thanks in
great measure to the efforts of CCA–Texas and the Texas Parks and
Wildlife Department. From May 1995 to May 1996, recreational anglers
in Texas landed an estimated 221,000 red drum within the 20- to 28-inch
legal size limit—almost 100,000 more than in the same period of
1990–1991, the period after killer freezes devastated the coastal fishery.
Texas anglers also landed 746,000 spotted seatrout of 15 inches and longer
in the same 1995–1996 period—an increase of more than half a million
fish over the 1990–1991 season.

In addition, Parks and Wildlife biologists say the average weight of
redfish retained by Texas anglers has increased from about 2 pounds in 1977

to an incredible 5 pounds in 1996. Success rates for spotted seatrout—better known in Texas as specks, or speckled trout—are also climbing, and the average creeled fish has doubled in size since 1974, to 1.9 pounds.

Since the Texas Parks and Wildlife Department, the Gulf Coast Conservation Association, and Central Power and Light Company teamed up in 1981 to build a hatchery in Corpus Christi, about 200 million redfish fry and fingerlings have been released in Texas bays. In 1993 the hatchery program produced and released 33.6 million red drum and 1.9 million spotted seatrout fingerlings. In 1994 a new hatchery was opened in Lake Jackson. The $11-million facility has an annual production capacity of 20 million fingerlings.

The fish are produced by natural spawning, using a photoperiod/temperature maturation cycle of 150 days. By carefully regulating light and temperature, biologists are able to simulate a year of seasons in five months. This creates two spawning sessions a year in tanks that hold two or three pairs of brood fish. Near the end of each cycle, the biologists simulate a fall cold front to induce egg laying.

Texas now has the "premier red drum fishery in the country," says Larry McEachron, science director of coastal fisheries for the TPWD. He says the goal of the hatchery program is enhancement rather than replacement. He notes that most red drum mortality occurs during the annual migrations from the Gulf of Mexico into the bays through the major passes. The stockings in the bays are intended to reduce the effects of that mortality and stabilize the highs and lows in recruitment. To build on these gains and ensure quality fishing for future generations, all Texas coastal anglers must be involved and vigilant. Killer freezes, algae blooms, and droughts are some of the natural forces that can adversely affect the fishery. Angler groups have little or no control over the whims of Mother Nature, but responsible anglers and citizens have proven that they can play a role in maintaining a high-quality fishery. A number of important issues must yet be addressed.

Freshwater Inflows

It may seem ironic that abundant fresh water is an essential element of a quality saltwater fishing experience; but according to Kevin Daniels, CCA's executive director, decreased freshwater inflow ranks near the top of the list of problems that must be addressed if the Texas coastal fishery is to thrive. Freshwater inflow to coastal estuaries is vital to the health of marine ecosystems. Studies by the Texas Parks and Wildlife Department show that virtually all of the fish and shellfish taken by commercial and recreational fishermen in Texas depend on estuaries for at least a portion of their life cycles. Key to the productivity of an estuary is the delicate balance between fresh and salt waters. Many of the organisms that depend on the estuaries cannot live either In totally fresh water or in water with high salinity. The 1996 drought in Texas, which raised salinity to levels that threatened marine nurseries, focused widespread public attention on freshwater inflows to estuaries. Floods, droughts, and hurricanes temporarily alter salinity, and even normal tidal movement can cause changes on a daily or hourly basis. However, industrial development has placed a longer-term strain on bays and estuaries. Stream channelization, water pollution, draining and filling of marshes, and dam construction are among the man-made factors affecting Texas estuaries. One of the many questions being discussed is how much fresh water is enough to maintain coastal marshes and grow shrimp, crabs, oysters, red drum, and trout.

About 80 percent of the fresh water entering Texas estuaries comes from river flows, which for the most part are controlled by dams on the state's major rivers. Freshwater inflow is therefore linked to the interests of many water rights holders such as farmers and cities as well as to those of sports anglers. The question remains whether the needs of the estuaries can be met in the face of increasing demands on Texas's water resources.

Aquaculture Issues

Texas fisheries officials have joined with angler and conservation groups in recent years to seek tougher guidelines on shrimp farms conducting operations on marine estuaries along the Texas coast. Coastal residents, anglers, and guides are demanding that polluted water containing silt, shrimp waste, and spoiled feed grains not be discharged into estuaries. Property owners filed a law suit in 1996 alleging that three shrimp farms had discharged polluted water into the Arroyo Colorado River and the lower Laguna Madre, a critical nursery for native shrimp and finfish.

Officials of the Texas Parks and Wildlife Department say questions remain about what happens to the food chain—the biota of a bay system— if large amounts of water are allowed to circulate through the shrimp farms. Questions must be answered about the quality of the water circulated back into the bays, and about the effects of suspended solids and other chemicals or byproducts carried in the water.

Another issue related to shrimp farms on coastal estuaries is the carrying capacity of an estuary as a supplier of water for industrial use. "There is only so much any estuary can cope with," say Parks and Wildlife Department officials.

CCA–Texas has suggested that the state should take a more aggressive role in reviewing permit applications as well as in assessing the impact of shrimp farm operations on adjacent bay systems.

*Unlucky finfish that become "waste" bycatch
from a shrimper's net near Rockport.*

Bay Shrimping Issues

In 1996, 1,871 bay shrimpboat license holders and 1,806 bait shrimp li
cense holders dragged their trawls through Texas bays and estuaries. Texas
marine fisheries officials and members of the shrimping industry were in
agreement that this was too many shrimpers chasing too few shrimp and
that unless the numbers were reduced significantly, the state's bay shrimping industry was headed for economic disaster. At the same time, a number of Texas anglers and guides, armed with evidence that bay shrimpers
were exacting a heavy toll on fragile inshore marine ecosystems, made the
case for removing all but bait shrimpers from these inshore waters.

For decades the bay shrimp boat had been one of the most colorful
and recognizable symbols of the Texas seascape. But in the eyes of some
users, the bay shrimp boat had come to symbolize a wasteful intrusion
upon Texas bays and estuaries. Texas Parks and Wildlife Department studies have shown that bay shrimpers kill four pounds of marine organisms
for every pound of shrimp harvested, with much of the discarded bycatch
being juvenile game fish. In addition to the concerns about bycatch, recreational anglers and guides worry that too many nets scar the bottoms of

bays, disturb sea grasses, stir up sediment, and generally disrupt the ability of bays and estuaries to function in their critical role as marine nurseries.

Working with the shrimping industry, the Parks and Wildlife Department, which has the authority under Texas law to set limits on when, where, and how shrimpers can conduct their business as well as how many can do it, has put into place a limited entry plan designed to address both the economic plight of the bay shrimper and the overharvesting of the resource. In 1996, the Texas Parks and Wildlife Commission set a moratorium on the sale of new bay shrimping licenses, which put a cap on the number of bay shrimpers in Texas. State law also gives the Parks and Wildlife Department the authority to further reduce the number of bay shrimpers by offering a buyback plan to the license holder. Funding for the plan is generated by sales of annual commercial shrimp licenses.

Angler Attitudes

Some anglers' attitudes about the harvesting of saltwater gamefish in Texas waters need adjusting, say Parks and Wildlife Department officials, and one of the best ways to change attitudes is through peer pressure.

This does not mean conservation-minded anglers should try to persuade others to throw back every trout and redfish they catch, says Gene McCarty, director of coastal fisheries for the Texas Parks and Wildlife Department. But it does mean being involved in putting a stop to illegal and unethical practices such as "double bagging" to exploit possession limits, or overfishing the deep holes that gamefish seek for refuge during and after a severe cold snap, just for the sake of filling coolers with fillets.

It also will mean changing the view held by some anglers that "a caught trout is a dead trout." TPWD's McCarty says it is a widely held view in Texas that it is always better to retain a legal-sized seatrout rather than return it to the water because seatrout are not hardy enough to survive the fight. He points out that a spotted seatrout is no more fragile than a rainbow trout caught in a mountain stream, and if handled properly, can be released to fight again. Such attitudes must change, McCarty says, because under the current harvest levels, the Texas coastal fishery cannot withstand an influx of many more anglers. He says there has not been a significant increase in the number of anglers fishing Texas waters in recent years, but the same anglers are taking more fish.

Whether the high quality of recreational fishing now enjoyed by flyfishers along the Texas coast is maintained will depend on the continued vigilance of dedicated anglers, responsible citizens, and progressive fisheries officials. "The question is, do we want to utilize this resource as a meat market, or do we want to use it as a recreational resource, or strike some balance between the two," McCarty says.

CHAPTER THREE

FLY FISHING THE FLATS

THE BASICS

Angler's Log
Holly Beach, Lower Laguna Madre
July 1989

As I walked along the sandbar, there she was with another big sow trout. The two fish were swimming behind a school of finger mullet. I made my cast to intersect them. This time the fly laid down where I wanted, just on the other side of the mullet. As the trout came into sight of the fly, I stripped once and it inhaled the fly. With a big crash, she was on and running.

I knew I had her, but for how long? My heart was beating faster with each run she made. As she made her runs I would run toward her to keep as little line out as possible. She would crash through schools of mullet. They were flying everywhere.

After twenty minutes, I knew the two-pound tippet couldn't take too much more. She finally started toward me, and I remembered all I had for a net was my left hand. I started shaking all over again.

As she rolled on her side, I pinned her behind the gills to the bottom. I left all the other trout and rushed to the weighmaster, and there it was—8 pounds, 11 ounces."

Chuck Scates, Rockport (on catching the spotted seatrout
that set the IGFA 2-pound tippet class record)

You stand vigilant, fly rod at the ready, on the bow of a flats boat being poled by a guide along the shoreline of a dead calm Aransas Bay. The guide suddenly announces in a guarded tone that there are three cruising redfish at eleven o'clock, fifty yards. ❧ Straining to pick out the shadows moving across the light sand bottom, you spot the three fish moving toward you and occasionally pausing to mill about. They are feeding and will probably jump on any fly that comes close. When they move into range, you deliver a tight, well-formed loop that lands the little shrimp pattern softly, just ahead and within the view of the lead fish. You impart a devilish little hop to the fly and watch as a fish surges over and pounces. You have the presence of mind to wait for the fish to turn and run. Then, with your line hand gripping the fly line, you set the hook once, twice, three times with firm, smooth, sideways motions of the rod.

This is the way events are supposed to play out on the flats. But often there are devilish puzzles to solve just as the fish show up. You might have to wait for the sun to shine through a bank of clouds. Floating grass might require you to forsake your favorite fly pattern. Or you might do everything right, only to have a loop of fly line wrap around the back of your reel just as that big red accelerates across the flat. When the adrenalin is flowing, there isn't an angler's guide, a casting clinic, or a fly-fishing seminar that can come to the rescue. Flyfishers have to gain flats savvy and confidence on their own, on the water in conditions that are both ideal and miserable.

Perhaps the biggest initial adjustment for flyfishers making the move from freshwater stream environments to the saltwater flats is in equipment and casting skills. Making accurate casts to moving fish, sometimes from a moving boat in windy conditions, requires skill in casting with rods matched to heavier lines—most often, in the 7- to 9-weight range. A sound casting technique is critical in producing the tight, well-formed loops and necessary line speed that enable the flats angler to make a 30-foot cast into 18-mph winds at moving targets, or 70-foot casts to the waving tails of redfish on a dead calm morning. But once the flats angler develops these casting skills, the game becomes a lot more fun. This is when the flyfisher stops worrying about how hard the wind is blowing and starts concentrating on where to find fish.

Armed with good casting skills, flyfishers will find the Texas flats open and accommodating. On most parts of the coast, all a flyfisher needs for hours of adventure on the flats is a road map of the area; an old pair of tennis shoes or wading boots; a 7- or 8-weight outfit matched with weight-forward, floating line; and a selection of small poppers, bendbacks, and shrimp or minnow patterns. To reach backcountry sites, a boat might also come in handy.

GETTING AROUND: FROM SKIFFS TO SEA KAYAKS

Shallow-draft boats perform best on the flats. A flat-bottomed johnboat with a 15-horsepower (hp) motor will deliver flyfishers to most productive shorelines with ease. These boats are quiet and will drift in very shallow water. Once you get to where the fish are, you can get out and wade instead of having someone pole you around the flat. Sea kayaks also are becoming popular for flats fishing along the Texas coast. With a sea kayak, you don't have to get in line at a crowded launch ramp. You only need a beachfront or roadside creek access to a bay system where you can pull off, park your car, and be on the water in minutes. The sea kayak can also be transported in center console fishing boats when it is necessary to traverse long stretches of open water to get to prime flats. And if the fish are stacked up in the corner of a lagoon where the bottom is too soft for wading, the kayak will get you to the fish.

Sea kayaks come in many designs that work well on the Texas flats. A good model for backcountry fishing is an open-cockpit, self-bailing, "no roll" model like the 14-foot Aquaterra Prism, made by Perception. This design has proven ideal for exploring backcountry tidal creeks, marshlands, and open flats. With a holder for a fly, spin, or baitcasting rod; a stick-on ruler for measuring fish; and storage space under two hatches for a soft cooler, camera equipment, and foul-weather gear, it is the perfect platform for the itinerant flats angler. The tough-skinned Prism is made of a thermoplastic linear polyethylene, weighs only 51 pounds and has proven extremely seaworthy in a variety of conditions. It travels well on top of a vehicle and is light enough to be launched single-handedly in minutes from a roadside access point. The craft responds to a light paddle stroke and easily cuts through the chop at the end of the day. The self-bailing design and airtight compartments provide buoyancy and stability, and the open cockpit allows easy entry and exit at the launch point or out on the water.

Another excellent craft for fishing the Texas flats, ideal for anglers who want to be able to stand up or use a trolling motor when on the water, is the Albion, a catamaran-style paddlecraft made by Mendocino Kayaks. It draws about 3 inches of water, is 11 feet long, 35 inches wide, and weighs 65 pounds.

Flats boats used for fly fishing should be as free as possible of obstructions such as cleats, ice chests, and other objects that fly line can wrap around. A towel soaked in water and thrown over a cleat or exposed fitting will solve this problem temporarily.

Poling Platforms

Poling platforms fixed to the stern of shallow-draft boats are a valuable asset on the Texas coast. Guides standing on these platforms normally will spot fish before the caster on the bow because they have the higher vantage point. The towers can spook fish, but only in slick, calm conditions or when fish are cruising an open flat and looking up for baitfish. Redfish will not be spooked by towers in the early morning light or midday light or when they are in a head-down feeding mode.

Tower platforms on the bow, with basket netting in front, enable fly-fishers to sightcast from a drifting boat during windy conditions. The basket is designed so that as the fly line is stripped in, it will lie at the caster's feet. With the wind, fly line usually will be pushed out in front of the boat. It is important that the caster strip all the line into the basket so that the line doesn't drag under the boat as it drifts along the flats. Smaller stripping baskets strapped around the waist are similarly useful in wadefishing, especially where there is floating grass and an irregular bottom with scattered shell.

WADEFISHING

Texas has an abundance of shallow flats with firm bottoms that are ideal for wadefishing. Wading a prime shoreline or grass flat by yourself—confronting the quarry in its own environment—is one of the purest pleasures of fly fishing on the Texas coast. It also is one of the most effective ways to take redfish, trout, black drum, flounder, and other flats species.

The most successful wadefishers imitate the slow, methodical movements of egrets, herons, and other wading birds that regularly take their meals on the Texas flats. Redfish and other gamefish are always on the alert for unusual sounds or disturbances. Corpus Christi fly-fishing guide John Mendleski cautions anglers to be especially careful when wading into the wind because it magnifies the sound of the water being displaced. If you can hear yourself making a disturbance in the water, you are going too fast, advises Port Mansfield guide Terry Neal. Neal advises his fly-fishing clients that if they can hear themselves wading, the fish can hear them too. When waders are in an area where the fish are active, if they just stand still, fish will pass within range. "I have fished days when I didn't cover 50 yards," Neal says. Another good approach, when waders find fish holding tight to the shore, is to get out of the water and walk along a section of shoreline to spot a target.

When wadefishing, anglers should always hold the fly by the hook-bend and have enough fly line—10 to 15 feet—outside the tip to enable them to quickly load the rod and cast in case fish appear suddenly. To become proficient, flycasters should practice casting with the wind on all quadrants to targets at a distance of 30 feet or less. In addition, although some anglers wading flats are comfortable allowing fly line to trail behind them the water, others might want to use a stripping basket, as there are many circumstances in which a trailing fly line can be a severe handicap. The ability to recognize changes in wind and current and to make quick adjustments, even if it means holding a few coils of fly line in the line hand, is a mark of the skilled wadefisher.

BLINDCASTING AND SIGHTCASTING

Many experienced saltwater flyfishers never make a cast when wading a shallow flat unless they sight a fish, preferring to concentrate on the hunt.

Making cast after cast over unproductive water can be exhausting and frustrating; but selective blindcasting should be a part of every flyfisher's flats strategy. Flyfishers should learn to recognize features that warrant a blind cast, such as creek mouths and dropoffs, channels, and depressions or "potholes" where light, sand bottoms are surrounded by grass. These are natural holding areas for gamefish. Likewise, any movement on the surface or disturbance around a bait school also warrants a cast.

EQUIPMENT, ACCESSORIES, AND ATTIRE

Sunglasses

A pair of high-quality polarized sunglasses is probably the single most essential piece of equipment for any angler setting out for a day on the water. Polarized lenses, preferably with side shields to keep reflected light from entering the eye, are essential for spotting gamefish moving across the flats.

There is much discussion among anglers about the best shade of Polaroids to choose for the Texas flats. Many experienced flyfishers give the edge to amber lenses for the high contrast they can provide against the dark backgrounds frequently encountered on the grass flats. Others say a brown tint offers a better balance between bright and dark days. Wearing a hat with a dark underbrim will enhance the effect of polarized glasses on bright days.

Line Clipper

Another essential tool for a day on the flats is a line clipper. A fingernail clipper purchased from a drug store works fine, or you can opt for a stainless steel version from a tackle store or catalog that comes with a retractable needle for clearing hook eyes. To avoid losing their clipper in the water, some anglers string it on a section of discarded flyline and wear it around the neck.

Clothing

Fast-drying, loose-fitting, long-sleeved shirts and pants made from a combination of cotton and nylon are the best choice for flats fishing.

Maps

Excellent fishing maps, which include coastwide high-altitude photography of bays, walk-in wadefishing areas, boating destinations, launch ramps, and marinas are available at most tackle stores. The maps, published by Shoreline Publishing (93337-B Katy Frwy., No. 176, Houston, TX 77024, phone 713-973-1627) and Top Spot (Pasadena Hot Spot, Inc., Pasadena, TX 77504) are available at most tackle stores in Texas.

Nautical charts of the Texas coast can be obtained from the National Oceanic and Atmospheric Administration (NOAA), U.S. Department of Commerce. Gaylord Stickle Co. & Assoc., Inc. (2715 Bissonnet, Houston, TX 77005, phone 713-529-8471) is an authorized agent for NOAA maps.

A Mariner's Atlas of the Texas Gulf Coast, by A. P. Balder, contains a complete set of charts for the waters from Sabine Pass to Brownsville. It is available in book stores and from the publisher, Lone Star Books (P.O. Box 2608, Houston, TX 77252).

The Roads of Texas (Shearer Publishing, 406 Post Oak Rd., Fredericksburg, TX 78624, phone 1-800-458-3808) and the *Texas Atlas & Gazetteer* (DeLorme Mapping, P.O. Box 298, Freeport, ME 04032) provide detailed maps of the entire state. The *Texas State Travel Guide* is available free from the Texas Department of Transportation (P.O. Box 5064, Austin, TX 78763, phone 1-800-452-9292).

TACKLE TIPS

Depending on wind conditions, fly rods as heavy as 9-weights and as light as 5-weights are effective for taking trout and redfish on the Texas flats. A 9-foot for 8-weight graphite rod matched with weight-forward floating line is probably the most versatile outfit for a day on the water. It can lay down a light leader with a #6 Crazy Charlie pattern or handle bulky crab patterns and poppers in the wind. It also will deliver the weighted Clousers and bendback patterns that work well around channels and dropoffs.

A 9-weight rod will do the job in a stiff wind, but it is a little heavy for casting over an entire day. A good quality 5-weight or 6-weight graphite rod offers the maximum in sport and can whip any redfish on the flats in short order. But in casting these lighter rods and lines, flyfishers sometimes lose accuracy and distance under windy conditions, especially in tricky crosswinds. It is important to have an 8-weight rod rigged and ready on those days that require a long stalk and a long cast to tailing and cruising fish that don't stay put for long.

A two-, three-, or four-piece 9-foot for 8-weight graphite fly rod matched with weight-forward, floating line on a single action fly reel equipped to hold 150 yards of Dacron or Micron backing is a good choice for redfish and trout on the Texas flats. Fly rods and reels vary widely in price depending on the weight and performance requirements of the buyer. The 9-foot for 8-weight St. Croix Legend, for example, retails around $200, whereas the 9-foot for 8-weight G. Loomis GLX is priced around $520. Reel choices include the Pflueger Medalist model 1595 1/2 fly reel with click drag and rim control ($34.50); the 3M Scientific Anglers System 2 fly reel with disc drag ($190); and the Abel 2 Big Game with anti-reverse ($520).

Sound Knots and Practical Leader Systems

Simplicity in knots and leader configurations is essential in saltwater fly fishing. There are numerous knot-tying books and references available to those less familiar with knot tying, such as *Practical Fishing Knots* (Kreh and Sosin, 1972). It's best to prepare tackle, clean fly lines, and build leaders before you get out on the water. The first stop where the redfish are tailing is no place to be constructing leaders. Learn a few good knots that you can tie when your sunglasses are caked with salt and the wind is blowing at 25 mph.

A sound, practical knot for connecting backing to reel, backing to fly line, and fly line to leader butt section is the Uni Knot, or Duncan Loop. For quick change convenience, many saltwater fly fishers put loops in each end of the fly line with a pair of nail knots. A loop formed with a Bimini Twist knot in the backing can be used to make a loop to loop connection with the fly line. Likewise, a Perfection Loop tied in the butt section of the leader makes a sound loop-to-loop connection at the other end of the fly line.

Leaders for the Texas flats should be roughly the same length as the fly rod being used. Flyfishers have the choice of buying knotless, tapered leaders or building their own by connecting lengths of monofilament. Some flyfishers prefer to buy knotless leaders because those with knots tend to pick up floating grass. Others say the knots in the homemade leaders are preferable because they shield the fly from the grass.

The Chico Fernandez leader configuration is ideal for the Texas coast. Use 5 feet of 30-pound monofilament for the butt section, 3 feet of 15-pound test for the middle, or hinge section, and 2 feet of 10-pound test for the tippet. For consistency, use the same brand of leader material for all sections. The leader-to-leader connections can be made with double surgeon's knots, blood knots, or Uni Knots. Among the most effective knots for connecting tippet to fly are the Duncan Loop, or Uni Knot, and Improved Clinch Knot.

Care of Equipment

Anodized saltwater reels are made to resist corrosion, but fly rods and reels exposed to salt air and salt water should be washed at the end of the day. Rinse with fresh water mixed with a mild soap or detergent. To remove caked salt crystals and maintain surface slickness, fly lines also should be cleaned after each day on the flats, if possible. Strip off the fly line into a sink filled with lukewarm water and a mild soap or detergent. Wipe the fly line dry with a clean cloth, then apply a modest amount of silicone-based line cleaner or Armor All to another rag and run the line through the silicone-coated cloth. Run the line back through a clean, dry cloth, and it will be ready to go back on the reel.

EFFECTIVE FLY PATTERNS FOR THE TEXAS COAST

Saltwater fish are opportunistic feeders, and many fly patterns work well on the Texas flats. Most guides choose simple, small, lightweight flies because they are easier to cast as well as to tie. Bigger flies will catch bigger fish in salt water, but it is difficult to position a large, wind-resistant fly when there is a 15- to 25-mph wind coming over your shoulder.

Small poppers from about 1 inch to 1 1/4 inches are effective on the Texas flats. Poppers larger than that are difficult to cast in the wind. The little 1 1/4 inch hard-body poppers tied on #4 stainless hooks that were developed by Houston fly-fishing outfitter Brooks Bouldin have become something of a phenomenon on the Texas flats. Although at first glance they look like something you'd cast to sunfish on a farm pond, a steady, short-strip retrieve on the flats produces the perfect gurgling action of the finger mullet that is such a popular food for redfish and trout. The little poppers in brown, yellow, or red are effective for blindcasting and sight-casting and often draw explosive strikes from redfish and trout. The East Cut popper designed by T. J. Neal of Port Mansfield is also an effective pattern on the Texas flats. On days when redfish are particularly skittish, Neal recommends no popping action on the fly but a steady retrieve that creates a small wake behind the popper.

Crab Patterns

Trout and redfish love small marsh crabs, so little crab patterns are effective, especially in the spring and early summer. Even the popping bug imitates a small crab up on the surface. When using this pattern, you can achieve a convincing gurgle action with a short, quick strip that makes the bug skip along the surface from side to side, in a zigzag motion. Some guides don't like to throw crab patterns because they find them difficult to tie and cumbersome to cast; but you will frequently find small crabs in the stomach of a redfish.

Capt. Scott Sommerlatte, a guide who fly fishes Matagorda Island's marsh lakes on the middle coast, has had great success with his Matagorda Fighting Blue Crab and Blue Crab Slider patterns. The Nix Crab and the Loring Baby Stingray/Crab are two other lightweight crab patterns that have proven effective on redfish.

A typical Texas coast angler's fly box.

Fly Patterns for Trout

Among the favorite foods of speckled trout are the croaker and the piggy perch, a member of the grunt family. Bendback fly patterns do a good job of imitating the piggy perch. Finger mullet 2 to 3 inches long are another favorite food of redfish and trout that can be imitated with deer hair and hackle feathers. Ron Mayfield, an accomplished fly tyer from Pearland, Texas, has designed a deer-hair pinperch imitation, part of his Mohawk Minnow series, that is effective with trout.

Effective Shrimp Patterns

The predominant shrimp species in the Texas bay systems, the white shrimp and the brown shrimp, are two of the best natural summertime baits. When these shrimp are being chased by redfish, they jump away, backward, faster than you can blink an eye. The best saltwater fly tyers think like a gamefish, tying shrimp patterns that can be worked backward, like a shrimp trying to get away from a redfish.

A number of shrimp patterns are popular on the Texas coast. When redfish are tailing in shallow water, or when trout and redfish are cruising or schooling in two to three feet of water, the most effective patterns are Cary's Crystal Shrimp, Brook's Shrimp, Nix's Shrimp, Scate's Shrimp, Sheka Rock Shrimp, Petrie Shrimp, and the Cactus Shrimp.

Small hard-bodied poppers are effective for trout and redfish.

Baitfish and Streamer Patterns

The Rattle Rouser, a bendback pattern with a built-in rattle, works well in murky water because it makes a clicking sound similar to the sound that shrimp make as they propel themselves through the water. Other effective minnow-type patterns for the Texas coast include the Chico's SeaDucer, Lefty's Deceiver, Dahlberg Diver, Clouser Deep Minnow, Grizzly Deceiver, Matt Hoover's Forty, Naiser Slider, Eric's Choice, Cary's Mud Minnow, Cypert Sea Tiger, Scates Hot Butt Bendback, Brooks' Wooly Hair Bug, and Cary's Saltwater Dahlberg.

Pick a Color, Any Color

Effective fly colors include red, pink, white, and chartreuse. On tough days when fish are not actively feeding, guides recommend natural colors such as light browns and greens.

Covering the Water Column: From Poppers to Clousers

Some flyfishers will say that you should use certain flies on certain days—for example, dark flies on overcast days and light-colored flies on clear, sunny days. But after watching redfish behavior on the Texas flats for years in different situations, we are convinced that color, size, and appearance don't matter much. If a fly is in the strike zone, the actively feeding fish is going to eat it. That is why having the right color is not as important as carrying a selection of flies that will cover the water column even if the water depth being fished varies only from 8 inches to 4 feet in the course of a day. That means carrying a selection that runs from poppers, slow-sinking shrimp patterns, and Seaducers to faster-sinking bendbacks and lead-eye Clousers.

Often, a bigger challenge than fly selection is making the proper cast and putting the fly in the strike zone of the fish. There are days when a guide will say "try this fly; no, let's try this one—no, this one" and go through every shade of color in the rainbow. On those days it often comes down to the ugliest fly in the box.

When Colors Do Count
There are shades of colors that seem to perform better in certain situations. In clear-water situations, guides will opt for darker patterns like red, whereas chartreuse, white, and pink sometimes do better in off-color water.

SKILLS TO BRING TO THE FLATS
Flycasting from a Flats Boat
Flycasting from a flats boat presents special challenges. The flycaster is moving because the boat is being pushed by the wind. The targets—gamefish—also are moving. In the time it takes for the angler to make the cast and begin stripping in the line, the boat has moved about 10 feet. So fishing from a drifting boat requires skill and timing in imparting action to the fly while keeping control of the fly line.

Identifying Gamefish on the Move
Different gamefish leave different signatures, called "muds," when they move along the soft sand and mud bottoms of the Texas flats. An ability to decipher these signatures gives flyfishers an advantage. A redfish will leave a "puff" of mud on either side. A flounder will make a series of boils. Trout usually leave a "slither" effect, with very little mud disturbance at all, but if a large trout is spooked, it will leave a puff or boil of mud.

Mullet are so prolific and so distracting on the flats that it is important to be able to separate them from redfish, trout, and other gamefish. When mullet move off the bottom without being alarmed, they leave a small stream of mud. Unfortunately, the mud boil made by a large mullet that is alarmed is very similar to that of a redfish.

When drifting through tidal marshes, it is important to rely on hearing as well as eyesight. Anglers should listen for the sounds that redfish make, especially at high tide, when they move into the grass along the shoreline. Anglers can learn to filter out the splashing of mullet and other baitfish from the more aggressive "popping" and "crashing" sounds of the redfish. When the wind is light, you can hear redfish hitting bait up in grass 1 foot to 2 feet tall.

Handling, Tagging, and Releasing Gamefish
One of the problems with trying to release larger fish in the bay systems is that if you fight them too long, they will become stressed and die, especially during the hot, summer months. If you are not planning on keeping a fish for the grill, try to get it back into the water as quickly as possible. During the spring, when the water temperatures hit highs around 75 to 78 degrees, anglers have a longer period to revive and release game fish. But in the heat of the summer, the fish decline rapidly.

Trout have a pair of canine teeth that are very sharp and very long. So anglers should not try to lip them like a redfish or a bass, because the trout will leave an imprint from those canines on a finger. Seatrout lose these canine teeth twice a year while spawning—in spring and late fall. Trout also have a thin membrane around their mouths that is about the thickness of tissue paper. That is why many fish are lost when they come up and shake their head during a fight. Seatrout are known to be less hardy than redfish, but handled with care, they can easily survive a landing and quick photo before release. Stainless steel hookouts, lipper gaffs, and the Boga Grip are excellent tools for releasing trout.

Flyfishers who land a trout in the 28-inch range—a fish of a lifetime, for most Texas anglers—are certainly justified in having the fish mounted. A photograph and accurate measurement is another option that will allow the angler to release the fish and still produce a lasting replica mount.

THE FISH OF THE FLATS
Red Drum
Because red drum, more commonly called redfish, are in such abundance and are such exciting targets in shallow water, more and more flyfishers are pursuing them on the Texas flats. For the flyfisher to be successful, it is important to know what to look for in the water. A waving, blue-tinged tail marked with a jet-black spot, or ocellus, is the most obvious and most dramatic giveaway, but there are also more subtle indications that can tip off the angler to the presence of redfish. Another easy way to spot redfish is to locate them cruising or feeding with their backs out of the water. Redfish are at home chasing prey in water only inches deep, so it is not uncommon to see a fish's back exposed up against a shoreline or in the middle of a tidal lake.

When redfish don't choose to expose their bodies in pursuit of prey, you can still spot them by the changes they make on the water's surface. A

A redfish cruising with back exposed in Corpus Christi Bay.

single fish often will create a V-shaped wake, and a school can generate a marked disturbance on the surface as it moves across a flat. Being able to identify this "nervous water" is important in getting properly positioned to make an accurate and productive cast.

Another way of reading the water for redfish is to look at the behavior of the forage fish. Baitfish act nervous, often jumping out of the water, when they are being shadowed or chased by predator fish. Another obvious way to spot redfish is by looking for fish "crashing" baitfish on the surface. When redfish are exploding on baitfish, they are likely to take any fly in the strike zone.

The redfish's mouth is aligned under its nose, which explains why it does much of its feeding off the bottom. In order for a redfish to take a popper off the surface in shallow water, it must rise out of the water. A flyfisher must avoid the tendency to pull the popper away from the fish in these situations. In water depths of 3 feet or more, a redfish is able to swim underneath the popper and grab it more easily. Popping bugs and surface flies therefore are more effective in deeper areas of the flats.

Spotted Seatrout
When stalking big trout in the early morning, look for V-shaped wakes on the surface. These appear when trout are cruising in shallow water and pushing water up over their backs. The mouth of the fish is 6 to 8 inches

An impressive speckled trout catch, preserved with a photo.

in front of the hump of the wake; so when casting, try to land the fly between 12 and 14 inches ahead of the wake.

Sightcasting to large speckled trout in the early morning is productive because they are active then and not as easily spooked. In the midday sun, wary trout can see a wader from a considerable distance.

Seatrout often move into water only inches deep, like redfish. Waders pursuing redfish might encounter an exposed back or tail that looks different, and it could very well be a trophy trout cruising and feeding in shallow water. The tail of a trout is more rounded on the sides than the redfish tail, which is a sharply defined triangle.

A mullet tail has a deep V in it, and when it is out of the water, it quivers. A tailing redfish will impart more of a flopping motion and leave the tail exposed, often for several seconds. Trout, in contrast, will not leave the caudal fin exposed nearly as long as a redfish.

A trout's mouth is configured in a way that allows the fish to feed on the surface. The bottom jaw is longer and the mouth is aligned with the fish's nose, so it can extend its jaw and come up and "pop" a baitfish or shrimp on the surface. Like a brown trout or a largemouth bass, seatrout will smack food on the surface and suck it down their throats.

Medium-sized trout will usually hang out on the flats around

30

The speckled trout, a surface and underwater feeder, has sharp teeth to capture and hold baitfish.

potholes—sandy depressions surrounded by submerged grass. Trout in the 1- to 3-pound range like the solitude in potholes, and they become very territorial and very aggressive. There are many pothole features on the flats of the Texas coast, and blindcasting into and around them can be very productive for trout and redfish.

Like redfish, trout also will tail on the flats and root around in the grass. During spawning periods, they act a lot like largemouth bass do when they start bedding. Trout will protect their holes with their lives; there are instances of trout with 15-inch mullet in their stomachs taking 6-inch flies off the surface.

Black Drum

The black drum is a flats dweller growing in popularity with flyfishers along the Texas coast. It has habits similar to those of the redfish but can reach 50 pounds or more in the bays. Black drum—or simply "drum," as they are called in Texas—are aggressive feeders but can be finicky when it comes to taking a fly. They tend to congregate on the flats in the fall in large schools, like redfish. Drum also will show in schools into the late winter and early spring. Their schools typically number between 100 and 1,000 fish, weighing between 5 and 50 pounds each. Drum are often found

This black drum was caught on Mustang Island, near Port Aransas.

around channel drop-offs. On the flats they live up to their name, drumming so loudly that sometimes you can hear and feel the vibrations through the hull of a boat. On the hook, black drum have a reputation for being tough battlers, making good use of their pectoral fins, which are longer than those on a redfish.

The population of black drum along the Texas coast is larger than it has been since the early 1970s, according to gill net samples by the Texas Parks and Wildlife Department. Black drum are not designated gamefish in Texas and commercial fishermen take them the year around.

"Puppy drum," in the 5-pound range, will tail on the flats and will sometimes take flies aggressively. Seeing the waving, squared-off tail of a black drum on a shallow flat can be as electrifying as seeing a redfish tail, and it's often difficult to tell the two apart. Smaller bonefish patterns on #4 and #6 hooks seem to work better on drum, and sometimes scaling down to a 6-pound tippet will draw more strikes.

It is best to target black drum over hard bottoms where you can get out and wade, because they are easily spooked around a boat. It also pays to keep a low profile when stalking these fish. They will displace water and make wakes just like redfish when they move across a shallow flat.

Ladyfish (Skipjack)

In Texas, ladyfish can turn up in bays, estuaries, channels, and flats and around piers and jetties from Sabine Pass to Port Isabel. They will take flies and other artificials aggressively and will take to the air when they are not making sizzling runs.

Ladyfish fill the Padre Island surf in vast numbers during the late summer and early fall, going on feeding sprees that in turn attract flocks of terns and gulls. Suggested fly patterns range from poppers to streamers to shrimp imitations. Durability is the most important quality in fly selection. It is a good idea to use a bite tippet for ladyfish. Twenty-pound monofilament is fine, but the line should be checked and retied often. Many flyfishers scale down to 5- and 6-weight rods to get the most fight out of ladyfish.

On the lower Laguna Madre, ladyfish can provide fast midday action after trout and redfish have dropped into deeper, cooler water, says South Padre Island guide Eric Glass. "I would venture that you cannot fish a whole day here in the summer and not hook a ladyfish," he says. "We don't have big freshwater inflows, but we have little tidal streams or guts that drain off barren, desolate flats. You can go up in them on a falling tide in the summer, when there is just a slight current trickling off the flat, and somehow a school of ladyfish has found it." Glass says he also looks for ladyfish on the back side of South Padre Island, where they patrol the edge

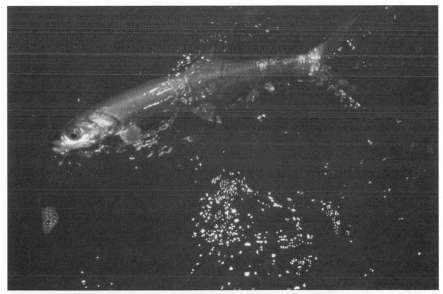

A ladyfish makes its way gracefully through the water at Port Aransas.

More and more anglers are casting flies to flounder.

of white sand flats in clear water. "They look like bonefish," he says. "They are hard to see and they run real fast."

Flounder

More and more Texas flyfishers are discovering how much fun it is to take flounder on a fly. They are learning where to find the fish and developing techniques to take them more frequently. Flounder get good reviews for their spunk on light tackle. "They are better fighters than trout and can be a load on an 8-weight," says Brad Smythe, a Rockport guide who frequently puts his fly-fishing clients on flounder.

A feeding flounder doesn't make a crashing sound, a big splash up on the shoreline. Instead, it does a flop on the surface. You can be poling down a bank line and something will catch your eye and it will be a flatfish doing the patented flounder flop. A strange sight, it is over in an instant and there is rarely a good long look. What the flounder is doing is flopping on a baitfish to stun it so that it can easily take it off the surface. Flounder often are found along the edges of channels and inlets and around troughs and depressions. Flyfishers often will spot flounder when they are being poled down shorelines.

Flounder don't always demand a tedious, bottom-bumping retrieve. They lie on the bottom waiting for their prey, but they can be as agile and aggressive in taking a fly as trout or redfish. With a serious set of teeth and a powerful tail that enables them to cover a short distance like a flash, flounder can compete for a passing fly on an equal scale with any other inshore gamefish. And like other gamefish, they have their moods, experts say. Sometimes you have to put the fly 5 inches in front of them, and other times they will go, as one guide put it, "from elevation zero to 4 feet in the blink of an eye" to get at your offering.

Rockport guide Smythe, who fishes the backcountry waters behind San Jose and Matagorda islands, tracks flounder movements by the tide and wind conditions. "When water is blown out of tidal lakes, flounder move off and stack up on shorelines behind barrier islands," he says. "It makes it much easer to take them on a fly because they are concentrated in shallow water on a specific shoreline." Flounder can be identified also by the mud that they stir up on a bottom. It is distinct from the mud made by a redfish or a seatrout. A departing redfish will make the mud boil and leave a mud streak on either side, whereas a trout will slither off, making only a slight disturbance in the mud. Flounder, in contrast, will make distinct puffs in the mud that look like a series of boils. Houston flyfisher Gonzalo Vargas says he looks for those signs when tracking big flounder around creek mouths along the lower Laguna Madre. "Sometimes you have to be very patient and get the fly within a 5-inch feeding range," Vargas says. "But if you see a mud puff, that is your flounder."

Any conversation on fly selections for flounder ultimately gets around to the Clouser Deep Minnow pattern. However, different conditions and different times of the year will dictate flies with different sink rates that can work the water column from top to bottom. Cary's Mud Minnow, designed by Dallas flyfisher Cary Marcus, is a fat-profiled fly tied with Krystal Flash that does an excellent job of imitating the killifish, a favorite target of flounder, especially during fall runs.

Finding flounder is always going to be the toughest riddle for the flyfisher to solve. But whether it's a 14-inch male or an 8-pound "saddle blanket" female, there are lots of flounder along the Texas coast, waiting on the bottom for the right fly to go by.

CHAPTER FOUR

UPPER COAST FLATS

SABINE LAKE TO FREEPORT

Angler's Log
West Galveston Bay
August 1995

*I pulled up to the grassy shoreline and waded out to inspect an inner arm
of the marsh. The spartina was tall and I'm short and in the march across
the grass, I tangled a loop of fly line in a bunch of weed. Standing in the
heat untangling the mess, I began to notice the splashing. Not mullet, not
flounder. More interesting splashes.*

*A redfish, rooting around for shrimp, waved its tail at me. There were
more splashes and more tails appeared across the shallow pond. I cautiously
stalked one of the tailing fish, dropped red and white streamers, gold
wobblers, and a white shrimp pattern in front of their noses. They either
ignored them or spooked off them.*

*Two hours later, I'm getting tired and frustrated. No fish has shown
interest in a fly. The sun is hot. The tails have stopped waving.*

*Just as I am about to quit, a wake comes toward me pushing up a
spray of fleeing shrimp. The mob of redfish is back churning almost at my
feet. I try a fly I've never had much confidence in—a bright red fuzzy shrimp.
It drops into the melee, and a redfish takes it. I strip set the hook and the red
tears off for the other end of the pond.*

I can't believe one of the miserable so-and-sos finally ate.

Tira Overstreet, Houston

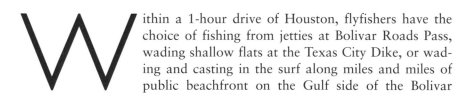

Within a 1-hour drive of Houston, flyfishers have the
choice of fishing from jetties at Bolivar Roads Pass,
wading shallow flats at the Texas City Dike, or wading and casting in the surf along miles and miles of
public beachfront on the Gulf side of the Bolivar

Peninsula and Galveston Island. The most dominant feature of the upper coast is the 600-square-mile Galveston Bay system, which includes Bolivar Roads Pass north of Galveston. San Luis Pass, the largest natural pass to the Gulf, separates Galveston Island from Follets Island, a barrier spit. A number of major Texas rivers including the Sabine, Trinity, Brazos, and Colorado enter the bay systems along this stretch of coast. Along the upper reaches of Sabine Lake near the mouth of the Sabine and Neches Rivers, where fresh water meets brackish bay water, it is possible for a flyfisher to hook a largemouth bass on one cast and a redfish on the next. Two of the Texas coast's eight major estuaries—the Sabine-Neches and Trinity–San Jacinto—are located on the upper coast, serving as rich nurseries for finfish and shrimp as well as a variety of birds. These semi-enclosed bodies of water receive vital freshwater inflows and are connected to the open Gulf.

On the upper Texas coast, a stiff wind is a frequent companion and sometimes a trip wrecker; but developing flycasting skills that can produce a tight, well-formed loop will carry the flyfisher through most days. The bay systems and waters near the shorelines of the upper coast are deeper and more exposed than those on the middle and lower coasts. Upper coast flyfishers should look for a sustained, moderate southeast wind that will push clear, green water along the bays and beachfronts from Galveston to Freeport. A stiff west wind that stretches flags straight on flagpoles will whip bay and Gulf water to an ugly coffee-colored froth unfit for the gaudiest Deceivers and Seaducers. Because the longshore currents on the upper coast carry large amounts of silt from the Mississippi, the bay waters here seldom have the clear, deep green that is seen on the southern end of the coast. Freshwater inflows, runoff from rivers, and occasional flooding also bring more frequent changes in water temperature than in the south. Water conditions on the upper coast are clearest during the winter months, when cooler temperatures dissipate suspended solids. With reduced boating activity, this makes winter an attractive season to fly fish the upper coast.

Being able to anticipate and capitalize on moving tides and moderate wind conditions is more critical on the upper coast than on the middle and lower coasts. And because of the vast stretches of open bays, offshore winds and tidal movements can have a greater impact on the upper coast for longer periods than on shorelines to the south. Flyfishers visiting the upper coast can obtain tips on tackle and effective fly patterns for Texas coastal fishing, as well as current information on fishing conditions, by visiting a number of specialized, well-equipped fly-fishing stores in Houston. Daily reports on upper coast fishing conditions also are published on the outdoors page of the *Houston Chronicle*. Published tide tables available at

The old lighthouse on the Sabine River at Sabine Pass.

local tackle stores also will help anglers identify the periods when gamefish are most likely to be ganging up at familiar haunts.

SABINE LAKE AREA

Keith Lake

Keith Lake is a small estuary off Sabine Lake with shallow grassbeds and shorelines that are ideal for wade- and driftfishing. It offers excellent drive-up access and walk-in wading or driftfishing from a skiff or kayak, and is a good choice for tailing redfish action during the fall. The shoreline is marked by mud banks and cane cover, with narrow canals on the Gulf side.

Most of the bottom at Keith Lake is firm enough to be waded, but some is soft and grabby around wading boots. The shoreline is protected even from prevailing southeast winds, making the estuary ideal for sight-casting from a kayak or a flat-bottomed boat in a variety of wind conditions. The Keith Lake Cut, a fish pass on the northeast end of the lake, offers good water movement during peak high and low tides. The fish pass is a good place to try a uniform sink line or shooting head to cut through the current. The tidal lake does not suffer from heavy boat traffic, but early morning wadefishers must share Keith Lake with duck hunters during winter months.

To get to Keith Lake take Texas 87 south of Port Arthur to Junior's Landing boat launch, on the right side of the road.

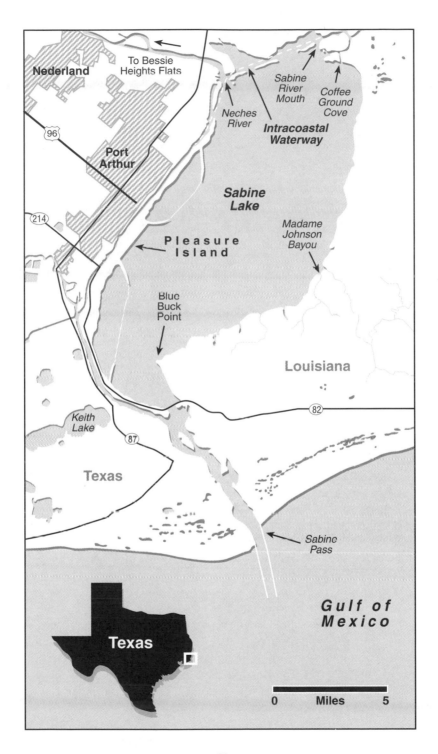

Nederland

To Bessie
Heights Flats

96

Port
Arthur

214

Neches
River

Sabine
River
Mouth

Coffee
Ground
Cove

Intracoastal
Waterway

Sabine
Lake

Madame
Johnson
Bayou

P l e a s u r e
I s l a n d

Blue
Buck
Point

Louisiana

82

Keith
Lake

87

Texas

Sabine
Pass

Texas

Gulf of
Mexico

0   Miles   5

Jack-up oil rigs near Sabine Pass.

Sabine Lake (North End)

In July, August, and September, when water temperatures begin to heat up in the cuts and bayous, flyfishers join other anglers in following flounder, redfish, and seatrout as they move out around the points in Sabine Lake, an expansive marine estuary 40 miles long and 13 miles wide.

Sabine Lake guide Skip James says prime times in the fall start about four days before the full moon in October and extend until late November. When the flounder begin migrating out of the bay in the fall, their movements can be abrupt and rapid, James says. "It is not gradual," he says. "We have gone to places in the first week of November and read the water temperature and salinity and caught the fire out of flounder. Then we have come back the next day, with the same conditions, and cannot make contact with them." James says flyfishers can do well on Sabine Lake in the fall. "If you can't find the flounder, you always have the redfish," he says.

Many anglers access Sabine Lake from marinas along the Sabine River at Orange. Proceeding down the river channel under oaks festooned with moss, you will pass refinery docks and spoil islands before entering Sabine Lake's north shoreline. This upper end of the estuary offers an excellent opportunity for blindcasting for schooling trout along the deeper channels as well as good driftfishing for redfish and flounder along the shorelines and bayou openings.

Look for good water movement, skittish baitfish, and shorebird activity around channel and creek mouths as a tip off to feeding gamefish. Sabine Lake fly-fishing guide Chuck Uzzle says a good indication that spring flounder action is about to begin comes when the mature alligators show up on the banks of the bayous. "That means the water temperature is coming up and gators and flounder are comfortable," Uzzle says. In addition to the alligator activity, flyfishers casting Deceivers and Clouser Deep Minnow patterns for flounder and redfish along the shorelines often are treated to the sight of otters, mink, feral hogs, and a variety of waterbirds including roseate spoonbills, white ibis, black-necked stilts, herons, and egrets.

Floating lines with weighted flies will work along the Sabine Lake bayous. For flounder, try prospecting with a shooting taper and a floating fly like a saltwater Dahlberg Diver with a short (3-foot) leader. After making a short strip, allow the fly to rise slightly before the next strip. Often a flounder will strike when the fly is rising.

Coffee Ground Cove to Blue Buck Point

The wild shoreline on the east (Louisiana) side of Sabine Lake, from *Coffee Ground Cove* about 16 miles south to *Blue Buck Point* on the southern end of the lake, is prime habitat for gamefish. Fish-holding features include cuts and finger islands similar to estuaries on the middle coast. There is constant water movement in and out of the marshes, and the creeks and bayous are rich in shrimp, mud minnows (killifish), bay anchovies, crabs, and juvenile finfish. Flounder hold around the eddies along the cuts on these shorelines on high tides and low tides. Flyfishers should look for the eddy points and cuts on these tides. Use "four-eyed" bead-chain Charlies and flies with lead eyes to get down in these currents.

Texas flyfishers headed into the bayous and cuts on the Louisiana side of Sabine Lake must have a Louisiana fishing license and saltwater stamp. You can reach this area by launching a skiff from the Causeway Bait Shop or the public launch ramp near the causeway bridge on the Louisiana side. Once the spring flounder migration is set off with a high tide during March or April, the reef area that runs from Pleasure Island to Madame Johnson Bayou on Sabine Lake is a prime upper coast area to fly fish for flounder. *Madame Johnson Bayou,* located on the east (Louisiana) shoreline of Sabine Lake, is one of the most prolific flounder fisheries on the Gulf Coast. Its shorelines are especially attractive to flyfishers because normal boating activity is only a fraction of that on the Galveston Bay complex. It is not uncommon for flyfishers to work the grassy shorelines for hours without seeing another boat. Little backcountry bridges that span the bayous provide another holding area for gamefish and are one of the few signs of civilization along Madame Johnson's winding shorelines.

It is not uncommon in March, April, and May on high tides in the morning to catch big numbers of male flounder entering the lake, says Sabine Lake guide Skip James. Through tagging studies he conducted, James found that local flounder trade into the Sabine Lake ecosystem in March, about four days before the full moon. James says they come through the Gulf pass and into the Intracoastal Waterway that feeds up along the western side of the lake. The fall migration is sudden and abrupt, whereas the spring migration of southern flounder is very gradual, James says. During the spring flounder run, the Causeway Bait Shop on the south end of Pleasure Island is well located to provide information on the movements of gamefish. "It is the first place where all gamefish stage," James says. Trout also migrate into Sabine Lake in the early spring months. James notes that every now and then anglers targeting flounder will locate nomadic trout running through the pass. "Throw a streamer in there and you may catch specks and reds," he says. During March and April James recommends that flyfishers work the south end of the lake because the salt content there is more favorable and the water is deeper. This area of the lake contains submerged rocks and other substructures as well as reefs with ridges and points going out into deep pools, challenging the flyfisher's casting skills. James advises flyfishers to use sinking lines and shooting heads around the deep drop-offs and reefs. By early May, flounder are fully distributed throughout Sabine Lake all the way up to the river mouth. "The water temperature is conducive to this movement and the photoperiod is long; all the reasons for them to be there are in place," James says. "And no matter what the runoff is, there is enough salt in the system."

On the west (Texas) side of Sabine Lake, on *Pleasure Island,* are embankment walls similar to jetties, with recreational piers and observation points. Wading along the outside rocks that border the deeper water, flyfishers find some of the best fishing on the lake at this time of year, local guides say. You can drive to many of these spots, walk out onto the rocks, and wadefish in waist deep water for redfish and trout that school in that area. Look for gulls and terns working over fish, or slicks from feeding fish in the spring and fall months.

From June through August, flounder continue their mass migration to the north end of Sabine Lake, chasing menhaden and other forage fish as they go. As water temperatures warm, flounder can be caught all along the banks of the lake. Especially large numbers of flatfish are found on "the

A speckled trout thrashes on the surface.

badlands," the more primitive and pristine shorelines on the Louisiana side of the lake.

Bessie Heights Flats

The *Bessie Heights Flats* are part of an estuary connected by a network of canals and bayous originally dug to provide access to marshland oil field sites on the Neches River between Beaumont and Orange. Its finger channels and backcountry shorelines are prime habitat for redfish, speckled trout, and flounder.

Veteran Sabine Lake guide Skip James says there is a big population of redfish on the Bessie Heights Flats, holding all the way up to the outfall of the Gulf States Power Plant. The warm-water discharge from the plant also makes this a productive fishing area during the winter months. James says the Windfree Ditch in Bessie Heights, a group of old pipelines and high spots that run in straight lines mostly parallel with the Neches River, is a good fish-holding feature with shell bars and deep drop-offs.

To get to the Bessie Heights Flats, launch a johnboat or shallow-water skiff at Port Neches Park. Proceeding upriver, there are two channel openings to the estuary, one 1/4 mile up on the right and another 1 mile up, also on the right. Each is about 12 feet deep.

EAST BAY SITES

Anahuac National Wildlife Refuge

The *Anahuac National Wildlife Refuge* covers 30,000 acres of brackish marshland. Located on the north shore of East Bay, its uncrowded, remote shorelines and bayous offer excellent redfish and trout action to flyfishers. Hard sand bottoms, grass flats, and scattered shell bars make the location ideal for wadefishing and sightcasting. Reefs extend well out into the bay. Boat traffic and angler activity are generally light around this remote refuge. There are 12 miles of graveled roads inside the refuge. Maps are available at the entrance, and signs direct visitors to the two boat launches and fishing areas. There is also walk-in wadefishing access to East Bay along Oyster Bayou Road. Fishing is permitted only in designated areas along East Bay bayous and shorelines. Visitors are asked to register when entering the refuge, but there is no admission fee.

You can "walk forever" on the Anahuac Refuge flats, says Galveston guide Chris Phillips. He recommends wadefishing during the fall months, when big schools of reds are known to patrol the shorelines. One good approach is to wade out in front of a stand of large cedar trees and work back along the shoreline. Near Frozen Point is a reef that can hold numbers of fish at this time of year. Anahuac's hard sand bottoms and sheltered shorelines make it an attractive wadefishing destination also during the winter.

The refuge is also a stopping point throughout the year for some 275 species of migratory birds. Between October and March, as many as twenty-seven kinds of ducks and five species of geese can be seen in the refuge. Herons, egrets, and ibis wade the shorelines. Alligators also are present and are most frequently viewed in the spring around Shoveler Pond in the northwest corner of the refuge. During the winter months, flyfishers hunting redfish and trout on East Bay shorelines are treated to the sight of some of the approximately 80,000 snow geese that stop off in the refuge each year.

To get to Anahuac's shorelines, travel east from Houston on I-10, then take exit 812 near the town of Hankamer and proceed south for 12.5 miles on Farm Road 61 and Farm Road 562. Turn left at the intersection of Farm Road 562 and Farm Road 1985 and proceed 4.2 miles on 1985 to the refuge entrance, then go right 3.0 miles to the check-in station. The refuge also can be reached from Texas 87 on the Bolivar Peninsula. At High Island, take Texas 124 north, then turn left on Farm Road 1985 and follow the signs to the refuge entrance.

Black's Reef Area

Galveston fly-fishing guide Chris Phillips calls the *Black's Reef* area, a shoreline that includes Little Pasture Cove and Marsh Point Flats on the

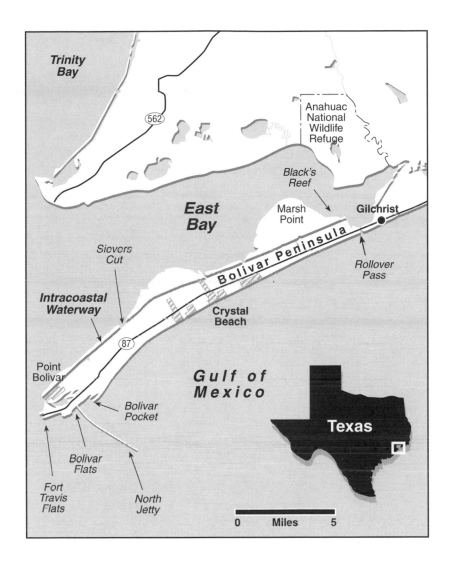

East Bay side of the Bolivar Peninsula near Rollover Pass, one of the best East Bay spots for taking large trout on fly tackle. Phillips recalls one fall trip when he and another flyfisher began seeing big trout cruising the area. They had to leave because there were too many other boats fishing the site. When they returned later in the afternoon, they found that the trout were still there but the boats were gone. "Everybody had left, but wading in the shallow water, we caught two 6-pound trout and missed some other huge fish that were cruising along the shoreline. It was like fishing Baffin Bay, with white sand bottoms up against the bank where you could sightcast," Phillips said.

Prime fly-fishing destinations in the Black's Reef area include Big Pasture Bayou, Sun Oil Lakes, and Rollover Pass's East Bay shoreline. The Sun Oil Cut once provided access to the shorelines along the *Sun Oil Lakes,* but it has been dammed up at both ends. Today you can reach these boggy lakes via Big Pasture Bayou. This is excellent redfish habitat, but the boggy bottom requires access with a kayak or small, shallow-draft skiff.

A short run across the Intracoastal Waterway in a johnboat or kayak also provides flyfishers access to prime wadefishing along the East Bay shoreline of Rollover Pass.

Black's Reef is located north of the Intracoastal Waterway and can be accessed by johnboat, kayak, or flats skiff from Lauderdale Public Boat Ramp near Rollover Pass.

Sievers Cut, below Elm Grove Point, is another good location for fly fishing that is accessible by boat. Around the corner from Sievers Cut are several remote tidal lakes that hold redfish. The shorelines along the high bluff area at the back end of East Bay also hold good numbers of trout and redfish.

Intracoastal Waterway Shoreline

Located on the Bolivar Peninsula across the Intracoastal Waterway from Shirley's Bait Camp, this stretch of shoreline is considered one of the best summertime wadefishing spots in the East Bay. Fish head for this shoreline in the evening, after holding during the day around East Bay gas wells and spoil islands. Local anglers call the site "the rips," which describes the bottom made up of many ridges and guts that attract fish to this shoreline. Flyfishers should arrive early to get a shot at fish cruising near the shoreline on moving tides. When the sun gets high, the fish bail out for deeper water.

Rollover Pass at Gilchrist

A man-made channel and fish pass linking the East Bay with the Gulf, Rollover Pass is another popular stop for anglers traveling Bolivar's Texas 87. Flyfishers can wade either side of the pass or cast from the bulkhead into the current, using Uniform Sink lines and weighted flies. Veteran upper coast flyfisher Ross Wilhite recommends wading the shell reefs along both sides of the Intracoastal Waterway on the east end of East Bay, near Rollover. He reports good redfish and trout action and light boat traffic on that end of the bay. Flyfishers also can wade the nearby beach and the bay side of the pass. Wading in the Gulf at the pass can be hazardous except at low tide, and a personal flotation device is essential.

Fort Travis Flats

You'll find redfish on the flats along the shoreline at Fort Travis, a World War II–era defense artillery installation, and jack crevalle chasing baitfish in nearby channels. The site includes a park with picnic tables and shower facilities. Wadefishing is good here in the summer months, especially early and late in the day. The area is protected from north winds and offers wadefishing and blindcasting opportunities in water from knee-deep to chest-deep levels. Life jackets are a must. Flyfishers also have the option of fishing from a boat around the deeper water off the southern boundary of Fort Travis. A submerged rock pile about 75 feet from the southwest corner of the park and 6 to 8 feet under water holds trout. Flyfishers should cast up-current and let Clouser Deep Minnow and Deceiver patterns swing over the rocks.

The Fort Travis flats are located 0.8 mile from the ferry landing on Bolivar Peninsula.

BOLIVAR PENINSULA

Bolivar Pocket and Bolivar Flats

The *Bolivar Pocket,* a protected estuary with a mix of hard sandbars and soft mud guts and a bountiful supply of gamefish, is located at the base of the north jetty on the Bolivar Peninsula. Water clarity usually is good over this protected flat even when westerly winds create sandy conditions on other Galveston area shorelines, though some anglers say the area is not as productive on days with prevailing southeast winds. Waders can blindcast the sandbars and guts for the reds, trout, and jackfish that chase baitfish over the flat on incoming tides. When wading the pocket, the closer you work toward the north jetty, the calmer and greener the water will be, says upper coast angler Layton Hobbs. He says flyfishers can wade, depending on how calm the water is in the pocket, to within 300 to 400 yards of the small boat cut, a channel opening in the north jetty that provides a short-cut for boaters traveling up the Bolivar beachfront.

Hobbs says flyfishers should cast around potholes and other depressions. He says that although these bottom features will change from year to year with wind and currents, typically bars and dips alternate with troughs. "Try to cast along those troughs, keeping the fly about a foot below the surface," he says. Often there are swarms of baitfish in the pocket. Watch for birds diving on feeding fish and work streamers around the edges or behind the baitfish schools for trout.

Seatrout are the most numerous species in the Pocket, with the occasional redfish showing up. Waders will hook sharks on occasion, and porpoises (Atlantic bottle-nose dolphin) also have been known to pay a visit.

*An angler casts from the north jetty at Bolivar Roads
Pass on the Bolivar Peninsula.*

Jack crevalle make their presence known by blowing up on baitfish, sometimes running school trout out of the area for a period.

An ideal time to fish the Pocket is in the heart of summer, Hobbs says.
Chartreuse Deceivers or Whistler patterns with small black specks that
match a productive Mirr-O-Lure plug are a good choice for blindcasting
here. Joe Deforke, another veteran upper coast flyfisher, recommends
Clouser Deep Minnow, Seaducer, and shrimp and crab patterns as well as
spoon flies and popping bugs.

To access the pocket, travel 4 miles from the ferry landing on Texas
87, then take the road on the right and proceed toward the beach. At the

beach, take another right and park by the barricades near the south end of the peninsula.

The *Bolivar Flats* also offer excellent drive-up, walk-in wadefishing prospects when incoming tides push in clear, green water. The Bolivar Flats are located along Texas 87 about 0.5 mile from the ferry landing. Waders may park on the roadside across from the Bolivar lighthouse.

TRINITY BAY/GALVESTON BAY AREAS

Trinity Bay (East Shoreline)

Trinity Bay's east shoreline is a productive area for trout and redfish in the spring and summer. Here flyfishers can blindcast from a drifting boat to schooling trout around slicks, or use shooting heads or uniform-density fly lines to sightcast to redfish crashing menhaden schools. Wadefishing also is productive in knee- to chest-deep water.

In the fall, menhaden schools along the shorelines and flats in front of Crawley's Seafood and McCollum Park will draw trout to this area. Look for birds attracted by baitfish pushed to the surface by schools of trout. Some of the better stretches are the areas in front of the marinas, which are reachable by skiff or sea kayak.

Small sites known to locals as *Redfish Island* and *Redfish Bar* are good for trout on calmer days in the spring, around Memorial Day. The flat gets shallow as it comes off the channel to hard shell bottoms in about 2 or 3 feet of water. Trout and redfish move through this area regularly.

Good wadefishing access is available at *McCollum Park* on Trinity Bay. The marsh areas and shorelines on the north end of Trinity Bay also offer attractive fly-fishing prospects. McCollum Park is located east of Baytown, off Texas 2354. Flyfishers can wade the park shoreline to the *Houston Lighting & Power* (HL&P) Company discharge canal, a prime winter fishing area. The bay here is deeper and maintains more stable temperatures than do shallower waters.

Galveston Bay (West Shoreline)

Kemah and Seabrook

The *Seabrook Flats* are located on the west shore of Galveston Bay, about an hour's drive southeast of Houston. Trout and redfish action picks up on these flats in the early morning and late in the day after northers or between fronts. Flyfishers should wade around piers and old pilings. The shoreline is protected against westerly winds. To get to the Seabrook Flats, take I-45 South to NASA Road 1 and turn right on Texas 146. You can access the Seabrook wadefishing area at Hester Street.

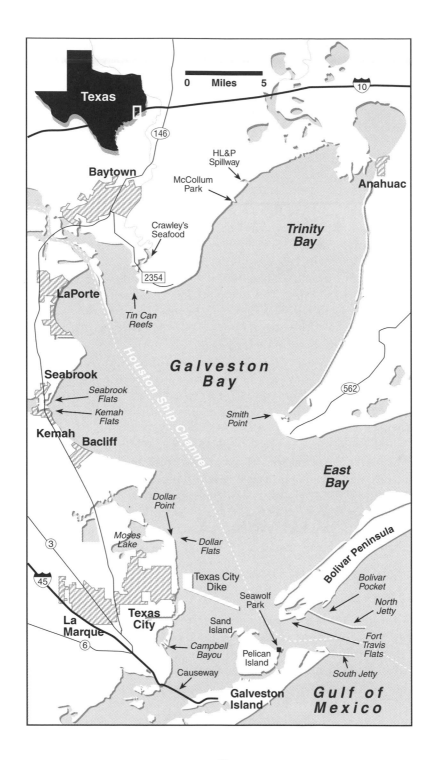

Texas

0 Miles 5

(10)

(146)

HL&P
Spillway

Baytown

McCollum
Park

Anahuac

Crawley's
Seafood

*Trinity
Bay*

2354

LaPorte

*Tin Can
Reefs*

Houston Ship Channel

*Galveston
Bay*

Seabrook

*Seabrook
Flats*

562

*Kemah
Flats*

Kemah

*Smith
Point*

Bacliff

*East
Bay*

*Dollar
Point*

*Moses
Lake*

*Dollar
Flats*

Bolivar Peninsula

(3)

*Bolivar
Pocket*

(45)

Texas City
Dike

Seawolf
Park

*North
Jetty*

La
Marque

Texas
City

*Sand
Island*

*Fort
Travis
Flats*

(6)

*Campbell
Bayou*

Pelican
Island

Causeway

South Jetty

Galveston
Island

*Gulf of
Mexico*

Good wadefishing also is available nearby on the *Kemah Flats,* on shorelines protected from northwest, southwest, and west winds.

Wadefishers also have the choice of fishing either side of *Dollar Point,* where incoming tides bring in baitfish. The area offers good fishing in summer, but the best fishing here is in fall and winter. The area also is ideal for casting around deep holes out of sea kayaks.

Other productive features nearby include *Moses Lake,* known for good fall and winter fishing, where reds hold in deeper holes, and *Campbell Bayou,* located on the mainland side of Galveston Bay, just north of Virginia Point. Campbell Bayou has a shallow shell ridge extending from the shoreline that makes it suitable for wading or driftfishing, and it is one of the few sites in the Galveston Bay complex that stay fishable during a hard northwesterly wind. Look for trout out deep and redfish up near the grass. Flyfishers also can do well on the backside of *Sand Island,* especially with flounder action in the fall after a cold front passes through. Here the shoreline is well protected from the north wind. The cordgrass shoreline also holds redfish, says Galveston Bay fly-fishing guide Chris Phillips.

The more secluded back (west) side of *Pelican Island* is a top choice of flyfishers because there is less angler activity there. It is a good area for reds and trout. Tarpon also are known to enter the bay in this location, where water depth increases to about 10 feet. There is little or no boat traffic here on the open water, and the bottom is smooth, hard sand.

Seawolf Park also is popular with many anglers in this area. The shoreline that runs from the back (west) side of the park to the causeway is a good wading area on south, southeast, or southwesterly winds. Features include shell reefs, grass, and hard sand bottoms. Fish this area on incoming tides and wadefish near the channel edges. Wadefishers can find solitude on this quiet side of the park. To get to this shoreline, take the wellhead road after crossing the bridge. Travel through the big iron gate on the paved road, which later turns into a shell road, and proceed to the back (west) side of the island.

Texas City Area

Texas City Dike and Flats

Only an hour's drive from Houston, the *Texas City Dike* offers flyfishers the opportunity to wadefish shallow flats that hold redfish or to cast off the rocks to Spanish mackerel and jack crevalle. The best wadefishing is on the north side of the dike, where there is walk-in access as well as boat ramps at a variety of bait camps. The area often is crowded on summer weekends, but there are enough broad, hard-bottomed flats and shorelines, drop-offs, holes, and spoil islands to go around. A good place to start is on the north side at the base of the dike, where there are a series of small spoil islands, hard sand bottoms, and a couple of shrimpboat wrecks. Trout are the primary target on the flats side of the dike, and jack crevalle sometimes get within casting range along the rocks on the south, channel side.

The sand spits and spoil islands near the dike hold fish in high winds. Waders can walk from spoil island to spoil island, casting around the deeper holes and depressions. Look for baitfish moving in clouds. Currents can be swift, and a life jacket here is mandatory.

The area also provides good winter fishing for flyfishers who don't want to contend with the summer crowds: There are flats and a deep channel near the boat basin. To get there, drive to the base of the dike and stop at the park. Pick a warm winter day to fish the flats. Look for changes in water color and cast to deeper water with big Seaducers, Deceivers, and bendback patterns.

The Texas City Dike and flats are about an hour's drive from Houston. Take I-45 (Gulf Freeway) southeast toward Galveston, to the Texas City exit. Follow the signs through town to the Texas City Dike.

West Bay (North Shoreline)

Jones Bay

Jones Bay, more commonly known as Jones Lake, is located near the north end of the Galveston Island causeway bridge. It is a good choice when high winds blow out other West Bay shorelines. Anglers tend to pass up this site, but the fishing can be excellent here in fall and winter months, as the bay is sheltered from north winds. It is easy to get to by walking up the railroad tracks near Fat Boy's Marina, off I-45 on the north side of the causeway bridge. There are places to park at Tubby's Crossing, near the bridge. The best time to wade this area is on a strong incoming tide when you can sometimes see fish moving in.

At the *John Mecom Marina and Subdivision,* located west of Jones Bay near Mecom's Cut, there is a series of 100-yard-long and 12-foot-deep levees. Mecom's Cut is a good winter venue that draws fish off the Intracoastal Waterway. The banks are high, offering protection from stiff winds in the dead of winter, and the water is relatively deep.

Green's Lake is another good West Bay choice when there are high winds. A small cut runs from Green's Lake to the upper shoreline of West Bay. Fish are caught in the cut and on the open bay in front of the cut. Cast Deceivers and Clousers near schools of baitfish. Look for trout slicks—the large, oil-like slick finish on the surface of the water created by feeding trout regurgitating baitfish. The slicks give off the odor of fresh watermelon. Driftfishing with a shooting head and a stripping basket is a good

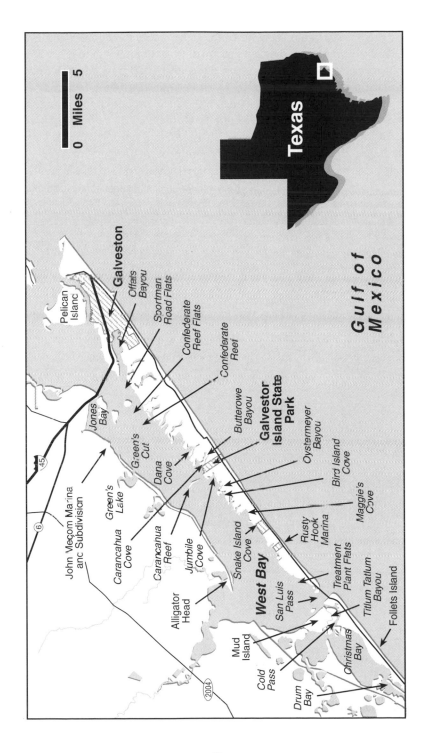

53

tactic here. A drawback for flyfishers is that the area gets mentioned in newspaper fishing reports frequently and often draws a crowd.

Nearby *Alligator Head* offers good wadefishing for trout and reds around the spoil banks lining the Intracoastal Waterway. It is located on the north shoreline of West Bay, just east of the mouth of Chocolate Bay.

West Bay (South Shoreline)

Offats Bayou, located inside Teichman Point on the upper end of the south shoreline, is an excellent winter fishing destination because of its many deep holes and reefs. It attracts heavy fishing and boating pressure during the summer months.

Walk-in wadefishing over firm sand bottoms can be accessed at *Sportsman Road Flats,* where there are shrimpboat wrecks and other submerged structures. Reds and trout move across these flats with the tides. The productive shorelines and flats of South Deer Island and *Confederate Reef* are a short run by skiff or kayak from these flats. To get to Sportsman Road Flats, after crossing the Galveston causeway bridge on I-45 and entering Galveston, take the 61st Street exit south toward West Beach. At Seawall Boulevard, turn right and proceed along the beachfront to Eight Mile Road (Anderson Ways Road). At Eight Mile Road, turn right and proceed to West Galveston Bay. The road ends in a narrow peninsula with a launch ramp and baithouse.

The *Confederate Reef Flats* are another popular walk-in wadefishing area on West Bay's south shoreline. The shoreline and broad, open flats have a firm bottom ideal for wadefishing and are intersected by a number of small cuts and channels where trout congregate. "You can catch school trout 50 feet from where your car is parked," says veteran upper coast flyfisher Joe DeForke. Try small, hard-bodied poppers early, then switch to Deceivers and Clousers around the edges of cuts. The Confederate Reef Flats are located on Sportsman Road off Eight Mile Road (Anderson Ways Road).

Nearby *Confederate Reef* also holds trout in the winter months. It is shallow, making it ideal for fishing during warming periods in the winter. Flyfishers can anchor up and cast the edges of the reef or drift the area. Boaters should use caution when approaching, especially during low tide.

The West Bay shorelines of Galveston Island State Park are accessible by kayak or johnboat and offer drive-up, walk-in wadefishing near *Dana Cove* and *Carancahua Cove.* The park provides access to a variety of flats, bayous, and shorelines that are protected under varied wind conditions. Redfish, seatrout, and flounder move to the back ends of the coves on incoming tides. Fish the points on outgoing tides.

Dana Cove to Maggie's Cove

This series of protected coves and bayous off the West Bay offer some of the best habitat for fly fishing on the Galveston Bay system. A good strategy employed by experienced flyfishers is to fish points and back ends of bayous from Maggie's Cove eastward to Dana Cove on strong incoming tides, then fishing back toward San Luis Pass as the tide falls out.

Dana Cove, located in Galveston Island State Park east of Carancahua Cove and past Butterowe and Oak Bayous, has a firm bottom for wading and is known for holding school-size trout as well as larger trout and redfish.

Veteran upper coast flyfishers put Butterowe Bayou, a narrow, wind-protected creek opening to the bay, at the top of the list of prime, year-around fly-fishing destinations. Like other West Bay coves, it is best fished on a strong incoming tide. Cast to the grassy points along the bayou, where flounder will hold. Work the outside points and move out to the flats on the outgoing tide. Trout and redfish will target baitfish holding around the points on outgoing tides. Kayaks will get you to prime spots around this bayou and neighboring Jumbile, Carancahua, Oak, and Dana coves.

Carancahua Cove, another exceptional West Bay fly-fishing destination located in Galveston State Park, offers walk in wadefishing over firm bottoms. It has two reefs at the mouth of the cove with a hard sand bottom separating them. The bottom gets soft toward the back end of the cove and around several small channels.

Once a dominant reef and favorite fishing spot in the West Bay, *Carancahua Reef* has been worn down by oyster boat activity; but it can still be good for trout action. Flyfishers should work the edges of the reef where the bottom changes from mud to shell. There is good open-water driftfishing around the reefs. Shooting heads and stripping baskets are recommended for prospecting the deeper water here. The area is productive but also draws lots of boaters and anglers because it is frequently mentioned in fishing reports. Carancahua Reef is located in front of the Jamaica Beach subdivision and is accessible by boat from a number of marinas in the area.

Jumbile Cove, another favorite of veteran West Bay wadefishers for years, is located just west of the Jamaica Beach subdivision on the West Bay side of Galveston Island. It has a wide entrance that takes the brunt of a north wind but is an excellent choice in south or southeast winds. Jumbile offers first-rate trout, redfish, and flounder habitat with marshlands, hard sand bottoms, sandbars, and broad, open flats that connect with deeper cuts. These nearshore coves and cuts are among the most productive and accessible features on the West Bay and are ideally suited for wadefishing. It is important to wear a personal flotation device and to be cautious when crossing to opposite shorelines. Waders crossing these canals and cuts frequently encounter pockets of deep water, soft bottoms, and depressions.

Many anglers watch for bird activity on open flats, signaling that trout are feeding in the area. Also look for active baitfish and shrimp activity on the surface in the far, back reaches of coves and bayous. Redfish and flounder often will corner baitfish in small fingers of the coves. Sightcasting can be excellent during these active feeding periods, as waking and cruising redfish up to 30 inches long can be seen moving in and out of the coves in water 1 foot deep or less. The area also is a haven for southern flounder. It is fairly common in these coves to see the "flounder flop," an airborne maneuver used by the flatfish to round up and stun baitfish.

When the more open water in Jumbile Cove is muddied by north winds in late fall and winter, the shorelines of several adjacent narrow bayous provide alternative fishable water and protection from the wind. Gold spoon flies fished slow near the bottom have proven effective in these bayous and coves during late fall flounder runs.

You can access Jumbile by boat or kayak from launch ramps at Sea Isle or Jamaica Beach subdivisions.

Ostermeyer Bayou, another productive West Bay feature just west of Jumbile Cove, is a good winter fly-fishing destination, but anglers must share it with hunters during duck season, which typically runs from late October through mid-January. This bayou can also be reached by boat or kayak from launch ramps at Sea Isle or Jamaica Beach subdivisions.

Bird Island Cove offers a number of backcountry bayous that hold redfish, flounder, and trout but are virtually inaccessible to most boats and waders. The bottom is boggy, and most anglers settle for fishing the mouth of the cove. Prime areas can be reached by poling a johnboat or paddling a kayak into the back bayous. Maggie's Cove, a narrow, bayou-like feature just to the northeast of Bird Island Cove, also draws redfish and flounder and is ideal for flyfishers in small, flat-bottomed boats or kayaks.

Snake Island and *Snake Island Cove,* located just east of the Sea Isle development, are good features in which to prospect in fall and spring. In addition to shorelines and flats, there are tidal lakes along the cove that are not shown on local fishing maps. These are boggy and inaccessible to anglers traveling by boat, but kayaks work well here. Flyfishers should also work the point, a good ambush area for trout and redfish that is 5 or 6 feet deep. To access this area launch a boat or a kayak from the Sea Isle development.

The canal area behind Cold Pass Marina on Termini–San Luis Pass Road on Galveston Island is an excellent winter trout destination and is also good in the early morning and late afternoon in the summer. In winter the deep water in the canal can attract and hold large trout. "You don't even get your feet wet," says Galveston fly-fishing guide Chris Phillips. "You can almost cast across it." For kayakers, this area also offers a variety of fish-holding features including a boat channel and several spoil islands.

The *Treatment Plant Flats,* an access point to West Bay wadefishing near San Luis Pass, offer excellent sightcasting prospects over firm bottoms. These broad flats attract crowds of wadefishers, but most walk out into deeper water. Flyfishers should not pass up the sightcasting opportunities in calf-deep water along the shoreline. The flat draws a lot of baitfish activity and offers protection to flycasters from strong southeast winds.

To get to this broad expanse of West Bay flats and shoreline, turn right off Termini–San Luis Pass Road at the water treatment station before you get to the Vacek Bridge. Proceed down the graveled road to the parking lot next to the treatment plant. About 200 yards off the parking lot is walk-in access to the bay.

San Luis Pass Area

San Luis Pass, the largest natural pass on the Texas coast, has been revered by generations of upper coast anglers for its raw beauty, power, and explosive fishing. Flyfishers can get a piece of the action either in driftfishing from a boat or in wading the Galveston Island side, where there is a hard sand bottom and a gradual drop-off. Most of the pluggers and bait fishermen walk out from the shore to fish the "pocket-deep" water around the channel drop-off. But flyfishers should not pass up the shallow, calf-deep water nearer the shoreline, where numerous oyster reefs draw feeding redfish and seatrout.

Because of treacherous currents around the pass, first timers should stay in the vicinity of other waders or seek information on safe entry points at nearby marinas or bait shops. Always wear personal flotation devices when wading near passes and deep channels.

Wading the edges of the San Luis Pass channel, flyfishers use sinking lines and weighted flies as they join the pluggers targeting speckled trout in the 7- to 8-pound class. In addition to trout, reds, black drum, flounder, and other inshore species, the Gulfside pass area also attracts Spanish mackerel, bull reds, and tarpon.

The flats along West Bay on the Galveston side of the pass offer drive-up, walk-in wadefishing over hard sand bottoms.

Follets Island Area

Anglers should avoid wadefishing along the steep channel on the Follets Island side of San Luis Pass for a number of reasons. "I have fished it for years and never caught anything," says Galveston fly-fishing guide Chris Phillips. "It is real treacherous, real dangerous."

Cold Pass, a channel that links West Bay with Christmas Bay, is located just across the San Luis Pass bridge on Follets Island and can be accessed from a park and boat launch. Houston flyfishers Ken Brumbaugh and Bill Stoneberg use sea kayaks to prospect along the channel edges and bayous of Cold Pass for trout and flounder. Joe DeForke recommends casting around the cuts for trout and working the points for flounder. This channel can be accessed by skiff or kayak. Boat traffic is light despite the availability of trout, flounder, Spanish mackerel, and sand trout.

The features around the Cold Pass Marina on Follets Island include a long boat cut and a road leading to the entrance of Churchill Bayou and Cold Pass. Bottoms here vary from hard sand to boggy mud. The cut is deep enough to fish in both summer and winter and is a good choice for wadefishing on a south or southeast wind. The tide is not a big factor as long as it is moving. Drive to the end of the road and wade out on the flat to the edge of the channel.

There is a big mud flat next to a parking-lot access point to Cold Pass, near the San Luis County Park (the Old KOA Campground), and flyfishers can walk around the mud flat on the edge of a marsh and find hard sand bottoms. Galveston angler Layton Hobbs recommends locating the drop-off, then backing up about 90 feet and casting back toward the edge. "Many people stand right on the drop-off and miss the fish that are cruising and chasing baitfish along the shallow edge," he says. For trout action, let Clousers, bendbacks, and other weighted flies drop down 10 or 12 feet around the shell reefs along the drop-off. "The fish work up and down that drop-off, and you can find action there if you stick with it," Hobbs says. He doesn't recommend fishing this area unless there are signs of baitfish activity.

To access this area for wadefishing or boating, turn right at the San Luis County Park after crossing the Vacek Bridge onto Follets Island.

Titlum Tatlum Bayou is about a 10-minute paddle by kayak from the launch ramps at San Luis County Park, at the east end of Follets Island. Bill Stoneberg has had success throwing Clouser and mud minnow fly patterns in the fall along this narrow bayou. "We caught the tide right and basically just sat on the kayaks and drifted the whole bayou, catching reds and flounder all day long," Stoneberg says.

Located along the extreme western shoreline separating West Bay from Bastrop Bay, *Mud Island* offers good wadefishing opportunities. There is better water movement here than on middle bay reefs because of the proximity of San Luis Pass.

Paddling the tide flats in a sea kayak at Galveston Bay.

Christmas Bay

Christmas Bay is another favorite of area flyfishers because its clear, shallow grass flats and shell reefs offer excellent sightcasting opportunities the year around. Harboring abundant redfish, trout, black drum, flounder, and sheepshead as well as many species of wading birds, gulls, and terns, Christmas Bay affords the flyfisher one of the most engaging angling environments on the upper coast. In the summer, look for tailing and waking redfish along shorelines early and late in the day. At midday, look for trout working under birds out in the deeper water, or for redfish cruising the shell bars and cuts around Arcadia Reef at the southwest end of the bay. Beach roads on either end of Christmas Bay lead to drive-up wadefishing.

Redfish, black drum, and sheepshead provide exciting sightcasting targets in the late fall and early winter, when the water is clearest. Use smaller flies, such as a #6 or #8 snapping shrimp pattern, to entice a strike from these high-strung porgies decked out in convict's stripes. In the summer months, water temperatures can warm to the mid-80s, restricting the best fishing to the morning hours. Flyfishers should time their trips to Christmas Bay to coincide with strong tides that move gamefish into the back reaches of the little bay. Work slow-sinking shrimp patterns and small poppers along shorelines in the early hours, and as the day progresses, move out gradually to waist-deep water. Deceivers, bendbacks, and Clouser patterns are a good choice for blindcasting over the grass flats bordering the deeper water and around cuts.

A ramp for launching boats, as well as drive-up, walk-in wadefishing, is available at Christmas Bay Outfitters (formerly Sy's Bait Camp) on the west end of Christmas Bay. Look for the sign for the marina on the north side of County Road 257 (the Bluewater Highway), about 3.5 miles from the San Luis Pass Bridge on Follets Island. Another access point for wade-fishing is located 5.5 miles from the bridge. Take a right off County Road 257 to the subdivision road that runs past a group of houses on the south side of a boat cut. The road ends on the shoreline of Christmas Bay. Wade-fishers can walk the northeast shoreline toward Christmas Bay Outfitters or turn left and wade southwest toward Arcadia Reef and Rattlesnake Point. The bay is less than 2 miles across; but flyfishers will need a skiff or kayak to reach the north shoreline, which also offers prime gamefish habitat and opportunities for sightcasting over light sand and submerged grass bottoms.

Drum Bay
Drum Bay, a smaller estuary lying southwest of Christmas Bay, also offers drive-up wadefishing from several access roads off County Road 257. Redfish and trout hold around the shell bars and the cuts near the spoil islands.

FREEPORT AREA
Jones Lakes
The *Jones Lakes,* a series of seven tidal lakes located off the Intracoastal Waterway near the San Bernard National Wildlife Refuge, offer upper coast flyfishers a secluded, backcountry fly-fishing experience. The area can be accessed by johnboat or kayak from a public boat launch on the Intracoastal Waterway near the point where the San Bernard River meets the Gulf. The lakes hold swarms of finger mullet and other forage fish. Narrow channels, shell reefs, sandbars, and log jams of driftwood and tree limbs provide prime cover for gamefish and restrict boat traffic.

Intracoastal Waterway/San Bernard River
The shorelines of the *Intracoastal Waterway* and the mouth of the *San Bernard River* also offer flyfishers a variety of fish-holding features.

To get to the boat-launch access point to the Jones Lakes on the Intracoastal Waterway, take Texas 332 west of Lake Jackson. Continue on 332 across the Brazos River bridge to Texas 36. Proceed south on Texas 36

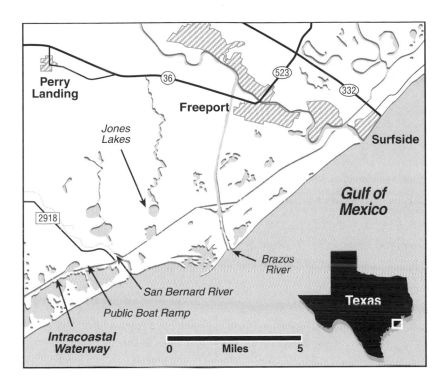

past Brazoria to Farm Road 2611. Bear left on 2611 and proceed to the San Bernard National Refuge. The road eventually runs into a public launch ramp on the Intracoastal Waterway. Flyfishers can launch a john-boat or kayak and proceed eastward on the Intracoastal Waterway. Cross the San Bernard River mouth and travel about 1.5 miles to the opening of Jones Lake No. 1, the largest of the lakes. Look for trout slicks around the points and the lake entrance. Jones Lake No. 1 is connected with the other six by a series of narrow bayous.

MIDDLE COAST FLATS

EAST MATAGORDA BAY TO THE UPPER LAGUNA MADRE

Angler's Log
North Shoreline, St. Charles Bay
September 1994

It was early morning in a blustery north wind when we entered one of the tidal lakes along the Aransas Wildlife Refuge by sea kayak. A gang of redfish was moving off the lake on a fast-falling tide. They were flying down the little creek channels, busting baitfish as they bailed out of the marsh. With gulls hovering over the feeding reds, we scrambled out of the kayaks and slogged through the mud so we could cast to them. Some coasted right by us. Some bumped into our legs. And some snapped up the bright orange Cactus Shrimp fly patterns we put in front of them.

Bruce Gillan, Houston

The middle part of the Texas coast offers the flyfisher miles and miles of clear, shallow flats where hunting skills can be as important as angling prowess. Thick, submerged grass beds, sand and mud bottoms, and shell reefs, trademarks of the middle coast, provide prime habitat for forage fish and crustaceans as well as the redfish, trout, black drum, flounder, and sheepshead that feed on them. The grass beds also filter and clear the water, providing ideal sightcasting opportunities.

This part of the coast is blessed with firm sand bottoms, and wadefishing is one of the most effective methods of stalking gamefish here. Middle coast flyfishers can wade the shores of barrier islands where whooping cranes spend their winters and where coyotes and wild hogs outnumber human inhabitants. The flats, tidal lakes, creek mouths, and channel drop-offs that cannot be accessed from beach roads or shorelines can be reached by small skiffs or flats boats from a host of public launch ramps and marinas.

Adding to the allure of the middle coast for flyfishers is the variety of attractive fish-holding features including bays, cuts, spoil islands, oyster reefs, and tidal lakes that stretch from Port O'Connor to the upper Laguna Madre near Corpus Christi. The region's barrier islands help shield this diverse habitat from the worst storms and give anglers a measure of protection from the relentless winds off the Gulf. Freshwater inflows from major river systems on one side of these estuaries and bay systems and deepwater passes on the other create and nurture these natural nursery areas and provide an escape route to the Gulf for myriad saltwater species.

Although the redfish has become the primary quarry here as elsewhere on the Texas coast, large solitary trout, black drum, sheepshead, flounder, and ladyfish also actively feed over the shallow flats. Healthy populations of redfish and seatrout, two of the most popular species on the Texas coast, cruise the flats, backcountry tidal lakes, and deeper bays. Often you can find aggressively feeding redfish tailing or wallowing against the cordgrass shorelines with their backs exposed, sometimes in water only ankle deep. That is when they offer the most exciting sightcasting targets for flyfishers.

Fly patterns popular on the shallow flats along this stretch of the coast include shrimp and SeaDucer patterns and small poppers in hook sizes from #2 to #6. Bead or lead-eye Clouser Deep Minnows are deadly around the channels, drop-offs, and jetty rocks, and Deceiver and Clouser patterns are effective in the surf.

Separated by deepwater passes at Port O'Connor and Port Aransas, the barrier islands that front the middle coast estuaries are Matagorda, San Jose, Mustang, and Padre islands. The rich middle coast fisheries and bird life are nurtured by five major estuaries—vital nurseries for shrimp, crabs, and finfish that are the food source for prolific gamefish populations. In the 1600s the Karankawa Indians—probably the first surf fishermen on these shores—smeared alligator fat on their bodies to ward off mosquitoes so they could harvest the rich marine life on the barrier islands.

The northernmost two islands in the main barrier chain, Matagorda and San Jose, can be reached only by boat. *Matagorda Island* is approximately 38 miles long and is bounded on the north by Pass Cavallo and on the south by Cedar Bayou. The northern two-thirds of the island is open to the public and is accessible from Port O'Connor. Primitive camping opportunities are available. A passenger crewboat operated by the Texas Parks and Wildlife Department provides round-trip service to the north end of the island. The south end of Matagorda Island is now managed as a national wildlife refuge and environmental research center. *San Jose Island* is bounded on the north by Cedar Bayou and on the south by Aransas Pass, a deepwater channel jettied in 1887 that tankers and freighters use as an entryway to reach the port of Corpus Christi.

The boat ramp at Goose Island State Park sees many early morning launches.

Mustang Island is separated from the southern tip of San Jose Island by the Aransas Pass jetties. The fishing resort town of Port Aransas is located on the northern end and is connected with the town of Aransas Pass by a ferry and a causeway and with Corpus Christi by a road down the center of the island, which connects with the John F. Kennedy Causeway. *Padre Island*, which stretches from Corpus Christi all the way to the Mexican border, is the longest barrier island in the world.

The middle Texas coast has a rich angling history that has been enhanced in recent years by the popularity of fly fishing on the shallow flats around Port O'Connor, Rockport, Port Aransas, and Corpus Christi. This locale's major attractions include the Aransas National Wildlife Refuge and the Padre Island National Seashore. A ferry operated by the Texas Parks and Wildlife Department at Port O'Connor takes anglers to fish the waters around Matagorda Island. Goose Island State Park near Rockport is one of the most popular jumping-off points for anglers in shallow-draft boats who are headed for the backcountry tidal lakes and shorelines around the refuges.

Among the middle coast institutions that have served anglers for decades are the Tarpon Inn at Port Aransas—a world-class fishing lodge at the turn of the century that is now listed on the register of historic places—and Kline's in Rockport, a popular restaurant where anglers and guides still gather for predawn breakfasts and strategy sessions.

The historic Tarpon Inn at Port Aransas.

The legendary Kline's Cafe in Rockport.

The arrival on the scene in recent years of Redfish Lodge on Copano Bay, a modern resort that caters to flyfishers, as well as J&J Tackle Town in Rockport and Gruene Outfitters in Corpus Christi—specialty tackle stores that have fully stocked lines of saltwater fly-fishing equipment—attests to the growing interest in saltwater fly fishing along the Texas coast.

EAST MATAGORDA BAY

Although East Matagorda Bay does not have a great amplitude of change in tidal movement on its flats, the north shoreline on the bay side of the Intracoastal Waterway and the south shoreline from the Redhouse Reef area to Brown Cedar Flats offers excellent wadefishing opportunities, says Jim Dailey of Palacios, a veteran middle coast flyfisher. The grassy shorelines here are wadable, attractive fly-fishing areas. Dailey recommends that flyfishers wading these flats work the edges of grass beds. There are good firm bottoms along the shorelines, and softer mud bottoms in the bayous. Dailey calls this "primo habitat" for reds, trout, and flounder.

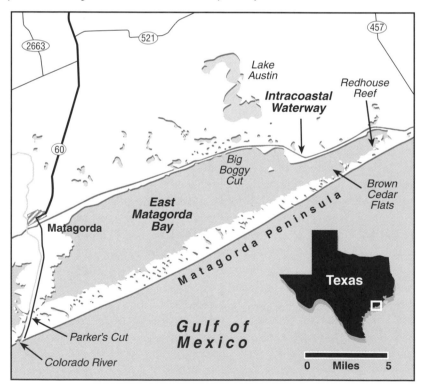

In the fall, when trout and reds are schooling and the birds are active, the fly-fishing action heats up along the East Matagorda Bay shorelines. Dailey says the north shoreline can be "an absolutely awesome fishery" on calm days or under north or northeast winds. The water is wadable and clear under these conditions and provides excellent sightcasting opportunities.

To reach the north shoreline of East Matagorda Bay, you can launch a skiff at Caney Creek Marina near the community of Sargent or at Chinquapin Bait Store along Live Oak Bayou. To reach Caney Creek Marina take Texas 457 south from Bay City.

The Colorado River at Matagorda

Many anglers describe the stretch of Colorado River that runs from Matagorda to the jettied Gulf pass as the best winter fishery in Texas. The point where the Colorado River meets the Gulf of Mexico is a particularly productive area for seatrout and redfish. Uniform-density, shooting-taper, or sink-tip fly lines should be used to deliver Deceiver and SeaDucer patterns to trout holding in the deeper water. Target the pass on days when winds are moderate, Gulf waters are calm, and the water is clear. Flyfishers can wade the shoreline near the point or take a kayak or johnboat across to fish the opposite shoreline.

To get to the mouth of the Colorado River, follow Farm Road 2031 from Matagorda along the river to the beach.

MATAGORDA BAY (WEST)

Parker's Cut

Once an opening on the Colorado River that provided access to Matagorda Bay, *Parker's Cut* has been sealed with an earthen dam. This protected area with light boat traffic contains a number of attractive bayous, flats, and drop-offs. Trout, redfish, and flounder hold along the shorelines, the bayou mouths, and the edges of the deeper channels. Although murky, off-color water is the rule over the mud and shell bottoms at the opening to Matagorda Bay west of Parker's Cut, there are pockets of clear water along the shoreline from Zipprian Bayou to Long Bayou.

Look for Parker's Cut on the right across the Colorado River as you travel by vehicle down Farm Road 2031, which runs along the east bank of the Colorado River toward the Gulf beach. Kayakers can park on the side of the road, paddle across the river to the cut, and with two or more people, portage a short distance to access the deep, clear channels and bayous that lie along West Bay's eastern shoreline.

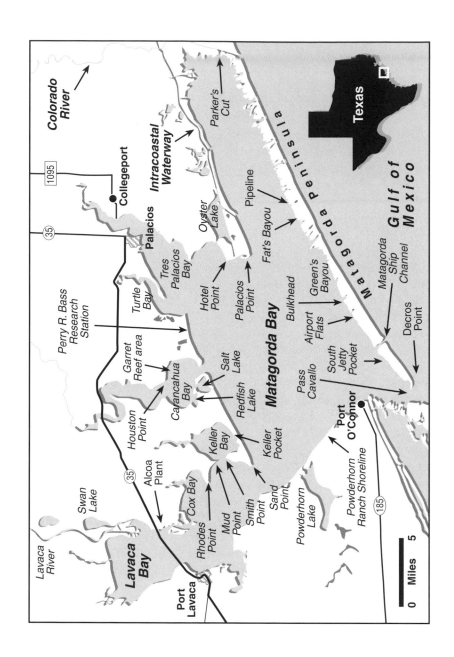

North Shoreline

The north shoreline of Matagorda Bay is another attractive wade-fishing locale. Trout and redfish hold on mud and sand bottoms along the shorelines, near reefs, and in coves. There is little submerged grass here, however, and water clarity during much of the year is sandy to muddy; but in the early spring and late fall when the water temperature is still cool, the water clears up, offering good sightcasting opportunities.

South Shoreline

The stretch of Matagorda Bay's southern shoreline from the *Pipeline* to *Airport Flats,* which includes Fat's Bayou and Green's Bayou, offers a rich mix of prime habitat for redfish, trout, black drum, flounder, and sheepshead. Flyfishers will find ideal wading and sightcasting opportunities for these species over expansive grass flats, sandbars, oyster beds, channels, submerged cuts, bayou mouths, and finger islands. The submerged grass bottoms along this stretch of shoreline provide prime habitat for gamefish. Look for fish holding in cuts and depressions and cruising fish over sandbars and grass flats. Anchor or stake out skiffs and wadefish shorelines and bayous.

In addition to redfish, trout, black drum, sheepshead, and flounder, jack crevalle in the 10- to 12-pound range occasionally pursue baitfish up on the edges of these shallow flats, with their big pectoral fins stretched out like outriggers.

Waders can walk well back into creek channels that cut deep into the peninsula to a point where you can hear the surf pounding on the Gulf beach side. Clouser Deep Minnow patterns or other flies with lead or bead chain eyes will take trout and flounder in the deeper channels and guts. There is a rich mix of forage fish, shrimp, blue crabs, and fiddler crabs along these channels and estuaries that constantly draws gamefish to this West Matagorda Bay shoreline.

It takes about 40 minutes, traveling by boat at about 30 mph, to reach this shoreline from marinas on the Colorado River at Matagorda, Texas. A shallow-draft, tunnel-drive or scooter-type flats skiff is required to negotiate the shallow, hard sand bottoms and oyster bars along many of these shorelines.

The *Bulkhead,* a breakwater feature, is located on the north shoreline of the Matagorda Peninsula near an abandoned military installation. Behind the Bulkhead is a small flat that frequently draws tailing redfish at sunrise. The Bulkhead is accessible by boat from launch ramps and marinas at Port O'Connor.

The stretch of shoreline from the *South Jetty Pocket* to *Decros Point* on the inside of the Matagorda Peninsula offers prime fly-fishing habitat with submerged grass beds and hard sand bottoms. It is a major path for gamefish moving in from the Gulf at Pass Cavallo, the Matagorda ship channel and jetties. This shoreline is accessible by boat from launch ramps and marinas at Port O'Connor.

PALACIOS–PORT LAVACA AREA
(See map on page 68.)

Tres Palacios Bay
Across Tres Palacios Bay from Palacios, on the bay's eastern shoreline, is a good wadefishing area that extends from the Collegeport community to *Oyster Lake.* There is no grass here, but shell bars are numerous. This shoreline is protected and holds clear water on a south or southeast wind. In the winter the plankton blooms subside, the water cools, and the sediments settle out very fast. From November through February, use uniform-density lines or shooting tapers to present flies to seatrout holding in deeper holes. Blindcasting in fairly shallow water along the shoreline is also productive in the winter. To reach this fishery, drive to downtown Palacios and step right off the seawall. Cast around the edges of shell bars.

The shoreline near Palacios—from *Palacios Point* to *Hotel Point*—is also a good wadefishing area. Flyfishers can walk in or access the site by skiff or kayak from the public boat launch near Palacios Bayou.

Also near Palacios is *Turtle Bay,* one of several small bay systems opening off Matagorda Bay. Turtle Bay is accessible by road, and flyfishers can walk in and wadefish, or put in a johnboat or kayak at the public ramp near Jensen Point. Water along this shore clears on light southeasterly or northerly winds.

Also accessible by road is the shoreline near the *Perry R. Bass Research Station.* Flyfishers can walk in to wade this area or launch a johnboat or kayak from Turtle Bay public launch ramp or marinas on Carancahua Bay. The cropped grass beds hold trout, redfish, flounder, and black drum. Parks and Wildlife Department biologists at the nearby research station confirm this as a quality fishery with regular sampling surveys.

Carancahua Bay
Located on the western shoreline near the mouth of Carancahua Bay are *Salt Lake* and *Redfish Lake,* two shallow tidal lakes that offer excellent wadefishing opportunities when they hold clear water. Salt Lake tends to be clearer and less boggy than its neighbor. These lakes can be accessed from nearby roads or by boat from the mouth of Carancahua Bay on the north end of Matagorda Bay. The nearest marina for launching skiffs and flats boats is at Ike's Bait Camp on Carancahua Bay.

Ken Geiger casting for redfish along a cordgrass shoreline.

Also close by are *Houston Point* and the *Garret Reef* area. Under favorable wind conditions, these features on Carancahua Bay offer an attractive option for fly fishing. You can drive to the shoreline and launch a kayak or walk in and wadefish. The area offers wadable bottoms that hold clear water around scattered shell reefs.

Keller Bay Area
The *Keller Pocket* has submerged grasses and offers exceptional wadefishing for trout, redfish, and flounder. Anglers can launch skiffs from several marinas and bait camps or from the state park nearby at Olivia. Midweek fishing is best because Keller Bay—especially this southwest pocket—attracts a lot of weekend boat traffic.

The shoreline along the stretch from *Mud Point* to *Rhodes Point* offers excellent wadefishing over firm bottoms and submerged grass beds. This stretch of shore is primarily a fall and winter fishery and is ideal on a north or northeast wind. The closest boat access is from marinas at the town of Olivia.

Cox Bay Area
The area from Rhodes Point to Husiache Cove and the Cox's Cove shoreline is wadable, with scattered shell bars that hold trout and redfish. There is no

submerged grass to clear the water here, but the location doesn't get much boat traffic, and the shorelines are protected on south and southeast winds.

The Upper Lavaca Bay Complex

The Alcoa plant complex offers exceptional winter fishing that attracts mostly the levelwind and plugger set, but it also is a good area to try shooting heads and uniform-density fly lines.

Flyfishers should also check out nearby *Swan Lake*. It has no submerged vegetation but a firm bottom for wadefishing. Good numbers of redfish hang around the shell bars. The lake also offers solitude because it doesn't attract much boating activity.

Lavaca River

Redfish hold near the banks on either side of Lavaca River. Access this uncrowded shoreline from marinas and ramps at Point Comfort and Lolita.

Lavaca Bay (West Shoreline)

This area, which extends from the public launch ramp at the park road access to the Lavaca Bay shoreline down to the public fishing pier at Noble Point, offers wadable shorelines. The site has no submerged grass, but it produces trout, reds, and flounder under low wind conditions.

Powderhorn Lake Area

Veteran flyfisher Jerry Loring puts *Powderhorn Lake* in the "sleeper" category. The treacherous shell banks and oil field structure around this lake require cautious navigation, but when the lake holds clear water, in the summer and fall, it draws good numbers of redfish. The north and south shorelines can be waded.

The east pocket of Powderhorn Lake has submerged grass beds and is protected from south and southeast winds. The north shoreline of the pocket is wadable, with a hard, sand bottom. Access points include Indianola Fishing Center and Powderhorn Recreation.

The *Powderhorn Ranch shoreline,* between Powderhorn Lake and Port O'Connor, offers excellent fly fishing for trout, redfish, and flounder. It is wadable over submerged grass, and it is protected from most winds, including strong south and southeast ones. From Port O'Connor, the shoreline is best accessed by kayak or boat due to the deep bayou just south of the Ranch shoreline. Anglers can put in from a number of Port O'Connor launch ramps.

PORT O'CONNOR AREA

The *Boggy Bayou* and Little Boggy shorelines near Port O'Connor offer drive-up, walk-in wadefishing and sightcasting to tailing redfish. Fish this area at sunrise and leave when boat traffic picks up. To reach Boggy Bayou, take Texas 185 to Port O'Connor. At Seventh Street turn left and proceed until the road dead-ends, then turn right. This road will take you to the shorelines of Boggy Bayou and Little Boggy.

Matagorda Island (Northeast End)

Bayucos Flat is among a number of small islands, estuaries, and grass flats that are a short distance by boat from Port O'Connor and offer prime wadefishing and sightcasting opportunities. These shallow flats and shorelines are ideal even on crowded weekends because you can run up a reasonable distance, drop your anchor, and then get out and wade areas removed from boat traffic. Bayucos Flat holds redfish and is a good place to stalk tailing fish in the morning.

Nearby *Whitacker's Flat,* located at the end of Saluria Bayou and continuing west, is another shallow, wadable stretch with grass beds. The back side of *Grass Island* also offers wadable flats that hold redfish, trout, as well as flounder.

Anglers who travel by boat around the point south of Grass Island can access tidal creeks into an area called *Big Pocket,* with a wadable shoreline that extends from Lighthouse Cove well into *Mule Slough*. It is important for waders in the slough to stay near the shoreline, where the bottom is firm. Out in the middle, in water 3 to 4 feet deep, the bottom can get soft. There are all kinds of small tidal lakes, cuts, coves, and bayous behind the shoreline that hold redfish.

Mule Slough also can be reached via Saluria Bayou. Once you reach the "J Hook," a point on a small island that opens into a shallow water estuary, you come to the entrance of Fish Pond. Turn around here and go back to the first cut that goes through the grass. Here you can anchor and walk into Mule Slough where there is excellent wadefishing.

Mule Slough and other nearby coves, bayous, shorelines, and tidal lakes make the Port O'Connor area an ideal fly-fishing destination.

ESPIRITU SANTO BAY (NORTH SHORELINE)
(See map on page 74.)

Located east of Port O'Connor near a cut that connects the Intracoastal Waterway with Espiritu Santo Bay is *Dewberry Island*. It is situated between the Lagoon and Espiritu Santo Bay and frequently draws redfish, trout, and flounder to its shorelines. During periods of spring tides, the small tidal lakes on Dewberry Island frequently pull reds off the deeper bay systems.

The nearby Intracoastal Waterway has stretches of grass that have been washed out around the edges by barge traffic, creating small cuts and

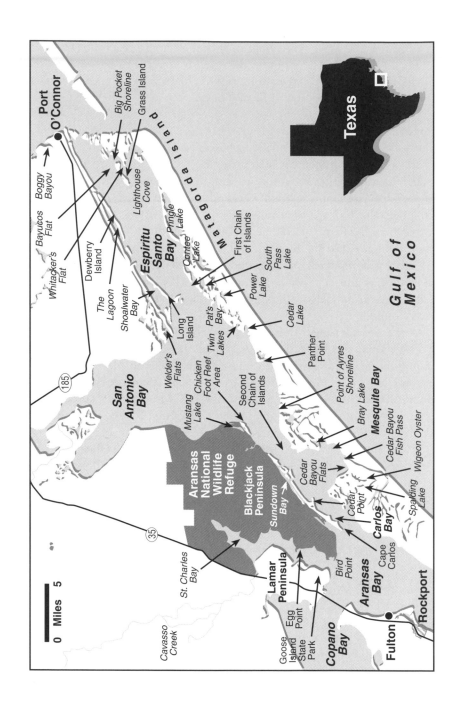

Texas

Gulf of Mexico

Port O'Connor

Bayucos Flat
Boggy Bayou
Whitaker's Flat
The Lagoon
Dewberry Island
Shoalwater Bay
Long Island
Welder's Flats
Mustang Lake
Chicken Foot Reef Area
San Antonio Bay

Big Pocket Shoreline
Grass Island
Lighthouse Cove
Espiritu Santo Bay
Pringle Lake
Contee Lake
First Chain of Islands
Power Lake
South Pass Lake
Pat's Bay
Twin Lakes
Cedar Lake
Panther Point
Point of Ayres Shoreline
Second Chain of Islands
Bray Lake
Mesquite Bay
Cedar Bayou Fish Pass
Wigeon Oyster

Matagorda Island

Aransas National Wildlife Refuge
Blackjack Peninsula
Sundown Bay
Cedar Bayou Flats
Cedar Point
Spalding Lake
Carlos Bay

St. Charles Bay
Cavasso Creek
Lamar Peninsula
Goose Island State Park
Egg Point
Bird Point
Cape Carlos
Aransas Bay
Copano Bay
Fulton
Rockport

185

35

0   Miles   5

74

drop-offs that also hold redfish, trout, and flounder. Work bendbacks and Clouser Deep Minnows around these holes. Dewberry Island is accessible by boat from the launch ramp at Charlie's Bait Camp and from marinas and launch ramps at Port O'Connor. Charlie's Bait Camp is located off Texas 185 east of Seadrift. Continue east on 185 for 6 miles. Turn right on Lane Road and proceed 4.5 miles. Charlie's Bait Camp is at the end of the road, on the Intracoastal Waterway.

On the north side of Dewberry Island is the *Lagoon,* a small estuary that includes a feature called the Berm—a large, bare sandbar about 50 yards wide and 400 yards long that lies a few inches under water. Under normal conditions, you cannot run a boat over this shallow bar, but it provides excellent sightcasting options for flyfishers wading on its hard sand bottom. The Lagoon is located along the Intracoastal Waterway between the Army Cut and Shoalwater Bay and is accessible from the launch ramp at Charlie's Bait Camp and from the marinas and the launch ramps at Port O'Connor.

Charlie's Bait Camp, on the mainland side of the Intracoastal Waterway, also provides access by flats boat or kayak to the nearby flats of Shoalwater Bay and Espiritu Santo Bay and of the Lagoon. These areas offer a wealth of wadefishing and sightcasting options.

Another prime area for wade- and driftfishing is nearby *Long Island,* which runs along the Intracoastal Waterway east of Dewberry Island. It is located between Espiritu Santo Bay and the Intracoastal Waterway and can be accessed by johnboat or kayak from Charlie's Bait Camp. Several cuts that empty into Shoalwater Bay and Espiritu Santo Bay along the shore of Long Island draw trout and redfish.

ESPIRITU SANTO BAY (SOUTH SHORELINE)
(See map on page 74.)

Pringle Lake
Pringle Lake provides excellent habitat for redfish and is a favorite wadefishing and sightcasting destination for flyfishers, being protected against the prevailing south southeast wind.

Shallow-draft skiffs can enter the lake and run in water of depths from 1 1/2 feet to 3 feet at the lake's middle. Veteran flyfisher Jerry Loring says he prefers to run his flats boat into the north pocket of Pringle, to a series of coves along the shoreline including Bird Cove, Bathtub Cove, Fencepost Cove, and the Rock Pile. All hold clear water over hard sand bottoms. Pringle Lake stays clear and shallow and offers a firm base for wading. From 50 to 100 feet out from the water line on the beach is a grassline. One of the best places to look for cruising and tailing redfish is where the light sand bottom meets the grass. The peak period to fish Pringle is from June to December.

An ideal time for sightcasting to redfish on Pringle Lake is from about 10 A.M. to 4 P.M., when the sun is more directly overhead. Most boaters who travel to Pringle Lake stay out in the middle and driftfish, leaving the shorelines to wadefishers.

When sightcasting to redfish on the south shoreline of Pringle Lake, waders must be extremely quiet and move slowly. The fish, which usually travel singly or in small groups of 20- to 24-inchers, are easily spooked in the clear, shallow water. Sometimes it takes an hour to cover 100 yards, Loring says. He says wading is productive as long as there is about 1 foot of water on the shoreline. When the water level drops below 1 foot on a low tide, the fish tend to move out into the middle of the estuary. Loring says big speckled trout also will move up on the Pringle Lake shorelines in April and May, and again in November and December.

The shoreline along the inside of Vanderveer Island on the Espiritu Santo Bay side of Pringle Lake can get boggy because the prevailing southeast wind pushes grass and other debris up against the shoreline. There is a cut at Rahal Bayou that allows boaters to exit Pringle Lake, but it is difficult to navigate because of extensive oyster bars.

About 100 yards past Rahal Bayou is a cut leading to *Contee Lake,* another prime wadefishing area on the back side of Matagorda Island. An excellent fishing site on Contee Lake lies just south of the main part of the lake, behind a series of finger islands. On a high tide, shallow-draft skiffs also can run from Contee back into Fifth Lake. This series of lakes can be productive for wading and sightcasting to redfish. Contee has rich grass beds that attract a variety of baitfish and shrimp, which in turn frequently draw the attention of gamefish.

SAN ANTONIO BAY (NORTHWEST SHORELINE)
(See map on page 74.)

Located along the San Antonio Bay shoreline of the Aransas National Wildlife Refuge is *Mustang Lake.* The entire upper end of this estuary has shallow, grass flats and hard sand bottoms that make for excellent wadefishing conditions. Mustang Lake is accessed by flats boat from the Intracoastal Waterway. Proceed north through the middle of the entrance to the cut, and then toward the upper end.

The *Chicken Foot Reef Area,* a multitude of oyster reefs in the middle of San Antonio Bay, offers productive blindcasting options for plentiful redfish and trout. Hopper's Landing, a marina near the entrance to the Aransas National Wildlife Refuge, is a good access point to these reefs. Flyfishers should target shell structure and points and use rattle flies, whistlers, and other attractor fly patterns when the water is slightly off-color around the reefs.

On calm days, when the water clears, anglers in flat-bottomed johnboats or shallow-running skiffs can see the many shell reefs in the middle of San Antonio Bay, which lie about 3 feet below the surface. During the winter months, trout leave the flats for the deeper water around these reefs.

SAN ANTONIO BAY (SOUTHEAST SHORELINE)
(See map on page 74.)

The First Chain of Islands (South Pass) is a group of protected islands on the lower San Antonio Bay. They have numerous lakes and offer excellent shoreline wadefishing over clear, hard sand bottoms. The area is known to attract good numbers of redfish.

Welder's Flats, an expansive area on the east side of San Antonio Bay, does not consistently hold clear water, but tailing redfish frequently show in early morning. Some areas are firm enough to wade and others are too soft, but there are excellent driftfishing prospects for flyfishers.

Close by, at the entrance to *South Pass Lake,* is a small cut that is well marked, and just to the right of it is a wide sandbar. Clear water holds behind the bar, providing excellent sightcasting habitat. Flyfishers can wade the entire island between the cut and South Pass Lake and have a good chance at trout and redfish. South Pass Lake is the first lake on the inside of South Pass Lake and is reached after exiting Contee Lake.

On a high tide, at the back of Pat's Bay, a little serpentine bayou runs straight into *Power Lake* and a horseshoe-shaped sandbar. Large redfish cruise this backcountry lake. Power Lake's bottoms can be soft and difficult to wade, but the shorelines are firm for the most part. Entry requires a shallow-draft boat because Power Lake never gets much deeper than 2 feet, out in the middle.

Leaving Power Lake and heading west down the San Antonio Bay shoreline of Matagorda Island, boaters will come to the *Twin Lakes,* tidal lakes that hold numbers of redfish and are excellent for fly fishing. Anchor at the mouths of these small tidal lakes and wade the shallow, grass flats and hard sand bottoms.

Just down from the Twin Lakes are the secluded shorelines of *Cedar Lake.* Cedar Lake has features similar to those of Pringle Lake, with hard sand bottoms and grasslines about 30 feet from the shore. This flat also provides prime habitat for cruising and feeding redfish.

From Panther Point to the Second Chain of Islands

The deeper tidal lakes are boggy in spots, but boaters who start at *Panther Point* and idle slowly northward will find an extensive shell reef that runs for about 3 miles. At normal tides, most of the reef is about 2 feet below the surface. The west side of the reef drops off to about 6 feet. This is an excellent place to cast shooting tapers or intermediate-density lines for trout holding along the reefs.

The stretch of shoreline from Panther Point to the *Second Chain of Islands* is good for wadefishing, with many channels and depressions. With its many small creeks, it is similar to Green's Bayou on the Matagorda Peninsula.

Boaters heading to the First Chain of Islands should also check out the *Point of Ayres* shoreline. Redfish will hold on this stretch of shore, which is good for wadefishing.

ARANSAS NATIONAL WILDLIFE REFUGE
(See map on page 74.)

About 30 miles north of Rockport off Texas 35 is the Aransas National Wildlife Refuge, an exciting fly-fishing destination. Several scenic flats on the 54,828-acre mainland portion of the refuge are open to roadside, walk-in wadefishing from April 15 through October 15, the period when the endangered whooping cranes that visit the refuge in winter are absent. During this period, anglers are allowed to wadefish several flats on San Antonio and St. Charles bays. Several points along San Antonio Bay, on the refuge's Tour Loop Road, offer excellent fly-fishing prospects.

Visitors also may park under the live oaks at the picnic area and walk across the road to fish the shoreline and grass flats of San Antonio Bay, or proceed to Dagger Point, where an observation platform with wooden stairs leads anglers down a sharp dune face to another broad San Antonio Bay flat. Both venues offer excellent wadefishing with hard sand bottoms, grass flats, and oyster reefs. Flycasters should practice the same techniques that work on the other shallow bay systems of the middle coast, trying a variety of poppers, streamers, and minnow patterns in ankle- to waist-deep water. If wind or water conditions prove too challenging at Dagger Point, anglers who obtain the required permit from the visitors' center have the option of traveling to the back side of the refuge, where there is access to wadefishing along the shorelines of the smaller St. Charles Bay.

The refuge is located north of Rockport near Austwell, off Texas 35. It is open 365 days a year from dawn to dusk. There is no fee for fishing, but visitors must register at the visitors' center.

A Spanish mackerel caught on a fly in the surf.

Matagorda Island (Southwest End)

Separated from the condominiums and beach traffic of neighboring Mustang and Padre islands by two channels and a barrier island, the shorelines, creeks, and tidal lakes of *Matagorda Island* offer a variety of excellent fly-fishing sites. The southwest end of this 38-mile-long barrier island, managed by the U.S. Fish and Wildlife Service as a unit of the Aransas Refuge, is not officially open to the public, but overnight camping on the beach near Cedar Bayou is permitted.

Once used by the French pirate Jean Lafitte as a hideout, *Cedar Bayou* is an excellent place to wadefish for reds and trout. In addition to the productive flats and channels inside this bayou, flyfishers also can try the surf side of the barrier islands. Casting Deceivers and Clouser Deep Minnows in the first or second guts on moving tides can produce reds, trout, Spanish mackerel, ladyfish, and jackfish. During the prized periods of favorable currents and light winds, waders in the surf often can see "bull" reds, in the 30-inch class, moving through the clear water, popping baitfish as they cruise the shallow troughs. For times like these it's handy to have a 9- or 10-weight outfit to throw 3- and 4-inch Deceivers, finger mullet flies, or Clouser Deep Minnows with bead chain eyes, tied on 1/0 and 2/0 hooks with a shooting head. The wreckage of several shrimp boats along the beachfront also makes for explosive fishing when the wind is light and the tide is moving. The aerial show alone is often worth a trip in the fall, says Neal Lillard, former manager of the Wynne Ranch on Matagorda Island, a onetime working cattle ranch. "When the huge schools of fry are pushed to the surface by the reds and trout, the avocets, cormorants, and white and brown pelicans go into a feeding frenzy," he says. "The water is alive with activity."

This end of Matagorda Island near Cedar Bayou is a popular area for anglers, who charter guides or make the trip in private boats from the Goose Island State Park public launch ramp near Rockport. Timing is everything at the bayou, says veteran fly-fishing guide Brad Smythe. Ideally, an angler must be on the scene a few days to see how conditions are developing. Among the favorable factors are light winds, incoming and outgoing tides, and green water close to the beach.

ST. CHARLES BAY
(See map on page 74.)

St. Charles Bay, known for large concentrations of speckled trout around its shallow reefs and redfish along its shorelines and tidal lakes, is lightly fished because of its remoteness and the profusion of oyster reefs, which discourage many boaters. Flyfishers will find that driftfishing from a skiff or getting out and wadefishing around the oyster reefs and spoil islands often result in high-quality redfish and speckled-trout action.

During the summer and fall months, redfish tails can be spotted on the north shoreline of St. Charles Bay, shining in the early morning sun.

St. Charles Bay (North Shoreline)
The eastern end of *Cavasso Creek* provides access by kayak or johnboat to the north end of St. Charles Bay and the shorelines and tidal lakes along the Aransas National Wildlife Refuge. Traveling eastward by skiff or kayak, flyfishers can wade the outside shorelines of St. Charles Bay or move into the tidal creeks and lakes along the refuge shorelines. Look for tailing and cruising redfish on shorelines, and work the deeper water and reefs of St. Charles for trout.

Shallow-draft boats and kayaks can be launched at the foot of the bridge where Cavasso Creek crosses Texas 35, 11 miles north of Rockport.

St. Charles Bay (East Shoreline)
Accessible from Goose Island State Park by flats boats and sea kayak, the shell reefs and narrow channels at the entrance to the St. Charles Bay are excellent for blindcasting for trout. The western side of *Blackjack Peninsula,* from *Egg Point* to *Bird Point* at the mouth of the bay holds good numbers

of redfish around its shorelines, coves, and creeks. The firm, light sand bottoms here are ideal for wadefishing and sightcasting. Fish this part of St. Charles Bay when the water is clear, on light to moderate winds.

Across St. Charles Bay from the Aransas National Wildlife Refuge, at *Goose Island State Park,* flyfishers can launch skiffs or charter guides for fishing some of the prime flats, creeks, and channels behind Matagorda and San Jose islands. To get to Goose Island State Park take Texas 35. Eight miles north of Rockport, turn east at Park Road 13. Follow the signs to the park entrance.

MESQUITE AND CARLOS BAYS
(See map on page 74.)

Thick grass beds and two large oyster reefs attract a lot of gamefish to *Cedar Bayou Flats,* near the fish pass that separates San Jose Island from the southern end of Matagorda Island. Accessible by flats boat, these flats have a firm bottom for wading, and their grass beds and shell reefs hold good numbers of redfish, especially on high tides—which is exactly when the access to this shoreline is easiest and when the fish are holding. The Cedar Bayou Flats don't get a lot of traffic from levelwind anglers because the grass makes lure fishing tough. They are ideal for flyfishing, especially with pencil poppers, Dahlberg Divers, and other small, hard-bodied poppers. Clouser Minnow patterns with bead eyes also work well.

Pluggers fish the deeper water and seldom wade the strip of water within a hundred yards of the shoreline. This is a good area for flyfishers to sightcast to tailing and cruising redfish.

Bray Lake
Bray Lake is well known for holding redfish. The reds have easy access into the lake from deeper water. There are stretches of soft bottom around the creek mouths, but boaters can run to the back ends of the creeks, shut down, and find firm bottoms for wading. Bray Lake attracts fish throughout the summer months and into the fall and winter. The far side of the tidal lake is the best side for fly fishing because baitfish move out along the shoreline when the tide falls out, and as the current turns, they circle the back end of the lake, where gamefish lie in wait for them. The best fishing is on a falling tide. Look for subtle water movement coming out of the creeks.

Blackjack Peninsula (Eastern Shoreline)
Blackjack Peninsula's eastern shoreline is a consistently productive area for redfish and trout that is often overlooked by many anglers. It has a firm, light sand and grass bottom. The critical factors for good year-around

fishing on the Blackjack shoreline are clear water and baitfish activity. The shoreline, part of the Aransas National Wildlife Refuge, is a short run by flats boat from the launch ramp at Goose Island State Park. It can be fished on the "inside" along the east shore of St. Charles Bay or on the "outside" along Dunham and Sundown bays.

Located off the Intracoastal Waterway along the southeast shoreline of the Blackjack Peninsula is *Sundown Bay*. This site can provide "awesome fly fishing," according to veteran middle coast flyfisher Jim Dailey. Shorelines on the inside of the waterway have submerged grass beds and are wadable. Sundown Bay is also accessible by boat from the launch ramp at Goose Island State Park.

From Cedar Point to Cape Carlos
Carlos Bay is a small bay system that offers excellent fly fishing on northeast winds. One of the more productive areas that is often ignored is the north shoreline of Carlos between Cedar Point and Cape Carlos. Fish-holding features here include scattered shell, drop-offs, and sand flats that offer excellent sightcasting options—especially during the fall months—for redfish and black drum. Boaters also can anchor on the south shore of Carlos Bay near Ballou Island and walk in to several very productive tidal lakes.

Located on the north end of San Jose Island, Carlos Bay is accessible by shallow-draft boat from Goose Island State Park.

COPANO BAY
(See map on page 83.)
The northeast end of Copano Bay around the Turtle Pen Lake area has an extensive flat that draws good numbers of trout. The best months to fly fish this area are early summer. The fishing picks up again in the fall. The northeast shoreline of Copano Bay has hard sand bottoms and is a prime wadefishing area.

From Redfish Point to Copano Village
The shoreline from *Redfish Point* south toward the community of Copano Village offers excellent wadefishing for redfish and trout over hard sand bottoms with scattered shell and grass beds in troughs. Waders also should inspect the series of small estuaries that open to the bay through small cuts. Just off this shoreline are shoals that also hold fish. Anchor up near these and wade or drift across them, casting near the edges. Piers along the shoreline around beach homes also hold fish, but wading around them can be difficult because of dredged channels and soft spots. Access Redfish Point shorelines by johnboat or kayak from Copano Bay Bridge Pier.

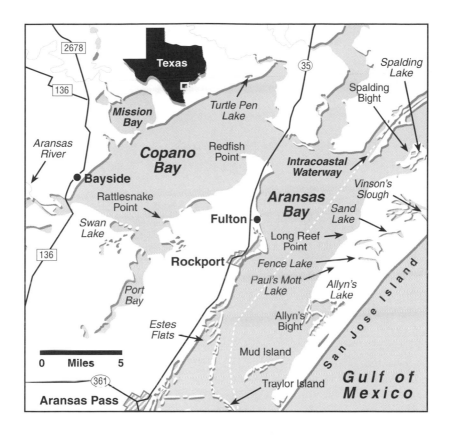

The Copano Bay shoreline around *Rattlesnake Point* also offers excellent wadefishing for trout and redfish over hard sand bottoms. A series of small lakes and tidal marshes to the south of Rattlesnake Point including Pete's Bend, James's Bend, and Italian Bend draw good numbers of redfish, black drum, and flounder. This area is rich in shrimp and forage fish, with abundant marshy flats that attract gamefish. Many of these marshes are fronted by private property and in some cases can be accessed only by boat. Some of these areas are open to wadefishing, but flyfishers should avoid crossing any fence lines into private property.

Port Bay, a small estuary on the southern end of Copano Bay, offers access to a number of productive shorelines and estuaries including Italian Bend, Pete's Bend, and James's Bend. Access this area by johnboat, shallow-draft skiff, or kayak from the launch ramp near the bridge that crosses Port Bay on Texas (Farm Road) 881.

Located just north of James's Bend in the back end of *Swan Lake* are a number of productive marshes that hold redfish. Swan Lake is accessible

Chuck Scates fighting a black drum on Marsh Flats, near Copano Bay.

by johnboat and kayak from launch ramps at Port Bay off Texas (Farm Road) 881 and at Bayside off Texas (Farm Road) 136.

The nearby shorelines and estuaries around the mouth of the *Aransas River* hold good numbers of redfish on high tides. Also, fish outer shorelines when the tide is falling out. Freshwater inflows into Copano Bay make this a prime shrimp estuary, which in turn draws the redfish to this area.

The Aransas River mouth at Bayside is accessed by johnboat or sea kayak from Glen's Marina near Egery Island and Egery Flats (Bayside Mud Flats).

Mission Bay
Mission Bay is treacherous for boating because of prolific shell bars, but it can be an excellent choice for fly fishing from kayaks because it holds redfish and does not get much fishing pressure. Kayakers can access the bay from the Mission River launch ramp, off Texas (Farm Road) 136.

SAN JOSE ISLAND
(See map on page 83.)
San Jose Island is bounded on the northwest by Cedar Bayou and on the southeast by Aransas Pass, a jettied channel to the Gulf that provides oceangoing tankers and freighters access to the port of Corpus Christi. The

The elegant reddish egret is part of the scenery at Copano Bay.

bayside and interior marshes of San Jose Island offer a multitude of shorelines, creeks, tidal lakes, as well as grass flats that are excellent for wading and sightcasting.

One of those features is *Vinson's Slough,* part of a series of remote, backcountry lakes connected by narrow guts within San Jose Island near the Cedar Bayou fish pass. It is virtually inaccessible except by airboat because of the distance from deeper water on the bay side of the barrier island. The easiest way to access it is with one of the airboat guides out of Goose Island State Park. Winding guts and bayous open into small, shallow tidal lakes with mostly firm bottoms and some scattered shell. Lakes can hold good numbers of redfish during the summer months. These lakes hold clear, shallow water, making Vinson's Slough a prime sightcasting destination.

Wigeon Oyster Lake is another remote tidal lake connected by a narrow creek to Vinson's Slough. The front part of it has a soft bottom. The best time to fish this lake is after a tidal surge, when the water level begins to ebb. Flyfishers access Wigeon Oyster Lake primarily from Goose Island State Park via chartered airboat with captains and guides experienced in fishing this area.

ARANSAS BAY (NORTHEAST SHORELINE)
(See map on page 83.)

Spalding Bight, a cove that offers productive wadefishing for redfish and trout, is located on the San Jose Island shoreline of Aransas Bay. Access Spalding Bight by boat from launch ramps at the Cove Harbor, Bahia Bay, and City by the Sea marinas, between Rockport and Aransas Pass. Next door to Spalding Bight is *Spalding Lake.* The best fishing here comes with high tides. A tipoff to redfish activity in Spalding Lake is the presence of stingrays. Often when the rays are moving across this lake, so are the redfish. Flyfishers who transport kayaks via shallow-draft flats boats can put out from the tidal creek near the entrance and paddle into the lake.

Located just south of Long Reef Point is a duck blind on a narrow gut that leads to a shallow tidal estuary known locally as *Sand Lake.* The lake is accessible only by airboat or by a shallow-draft flats boat with a skilled captain who knows the area. Boats can travel only part of the way up the narrow guts, and flyfishers must wade several hundred yards along the channel's soft bottoms to reach the lake. However, Sand Lake itself offers excellent wadefishing over firm bottoms, and draws good numbers of redfish and black drum from late summer into the fall.

Paul's Mott Lake, another of the many tidal lakes behind San Jose Island, often serves as a highway for redfish moving into *Fence Lake.* Located southwest of Jay Bird Point, Fence Lake is a broad tidal lake that frequently holds good numbers of redfish. It gets its name from the fence posts stretching across the middle of the flat. It has firm sand bottoms and grass beds, and the back end of the lake has a deeper channel that should always be checked out for redfish.

Also located on the San Jose Island shoreline along Aransas Bay is *Allyn's Bight,* another good area for redfish. Like all of the tidal lakes on the back side of San Jose Island, it can be accessed by boat from Rockport marinas. Nearby *Allyn's Lake* is the choice for flyfishers on high tides, when water levels in the estuary reach about 1 1/2 feet.

Mud Island, a dominant feature on the Lydia Ann Channel near the west shoreline of San Jose Island, offers flyfishers the opportunity to wade along channel drop-offs, blindcasting for trout along the deeper end and sightcasting to redfish on the flats side. The island is a straight shot down the Lydia Ann Channel from marinas and launch ramps at Port Aransas. *North Pass,* a shallow inlet carved into the back side of San Jose Island southeast of Mud Island, is surrounded on either side by a long stretch of firm, light sand bottom. The slight drop-off holds redfish and trout and the expansive flat offers firm footing, a light sand bottom, and good visibility for sightcasting to cruising fish.

ROCKPORT/FULTON AREA

Accessible from launch ramps in the Rockport/Fulton area, the shorelines of *Traylor Island* consistently hold trout and redfish drawn out of the deeper Lydia Ann Channel. Look for pods of redfish cruising near the bank around cuts and depressions, and cast near the channel drop-off for trout.

Located on Redfish Bay just off the Intracoastal Waterway between Rockport and Aransas Pass, *Estes Flats* offers wadefishing over broad, shallow flats with grass beds, oyster shells, spoil island banks, and small tidal creeks. These features consistently draw redfish, trout, flounder, and black drum. This is a popular area that also draws heavy boat traffic from nearby marinas, especially between spring and fall. A large spoil island on the north Estes Flats shoreline just down from the Palm Harbor launch ramp, across from Channel Marker 25, is an excellent wadefishing and sightcasting area for trout and redfish. Despite its ideal light sand bottoms, it is frequently passed up by anglers departing from nearby launch ramps.

PORT ARANSAS/ARANSAS PASS AREA

Since the late 1800s, when tourists from across the country first journeyed to Port Aransas by train and by boat to stay at the famous Tarpon Inn and to fish the nearby waters, this fishing and resort community has been a popular angling destination. Port Aransas provides easy boat and drive-up access to flats fishing on Aransas, Redfish, and Corpus Christi bays as well as opportunities for fishing from nearby jetties, beaches, passes, and the open Gulf. The community has a wide variety of lodging available at hotels, motels, and condos, including the old Tarpon Inn, whose rooms have been restored and remodeled in recent years.

Port Aransas is located on the northern end of Mustang Island and is connected with the town of Aransas Pass by ferry and causeway and with Corpus Christi by Texas 361. The town of Aransas Pass is located on Texas 35 between Rockport and Corpus Christi.

Causeway Road Area

Located on Redfish Bay, *Stedman Island* offers drive up, walk-in wadefishing for trout, redfish, flounder, and black drum. To reach the best wading

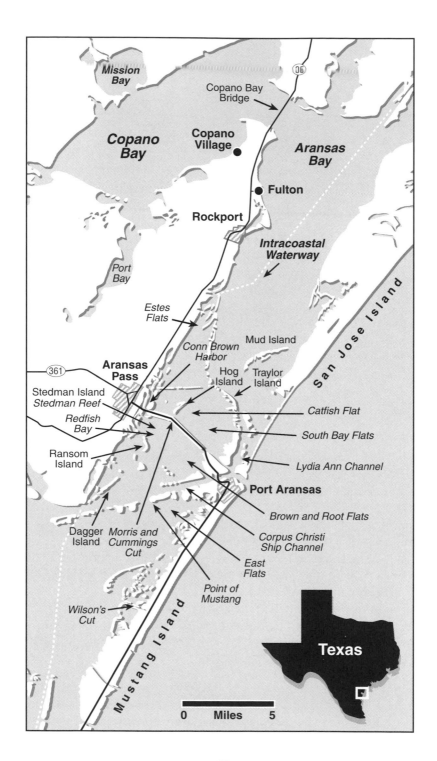

Mission Bay

Copano Bay Bridge

06

Copano Village

Copano Bay

Aransas Bay

Fulton

Rockport

Intracoastal Waterway

Port Bay

Estes Flats

Mud Island

Conn Brown Harbor

San Jose Island

Aransas Pass

361

Hog Island

Traylor Island

Stedman Island
Stedman Reef

Catfish Flat

Redfish Bay

South Bay Flats

Ransom Island

Lydia Ann Channel

Port Aransas

Brown and Root Flats

Dagger Island

Morris and Cummings Cut

Corpus Christi Ship Channel

East Flats

Point of Mustang

Wilson's Cut

Mustang Island

Texas

0   Miles   5

A flounder and fly, near Rockport.

sites by vehicle, take the wellpad roads near Fin and Feather Marina to the back side of the island. This is an ideal place to work a small popper on top or bounce a bendback around the edges of the oyster reefs and potholes. A visit at low tide will reveal numerous shell banks, small channels, and guts. The hard sand bottom is easily waded, well out into the bay. This flat is often alive with finger mullet, pinfish, shrimp, and small crabs that frequently draw the attention of passing reds, speckled trout, black drum, ladyfish, and flounder.

Although blindcasting is the normal drill for working these flats, fly-fishers should stay on the lookout for the V-shaped wakes of cruising redfish and the oily slicks characteristic of feeding seatrout. Any unusual wave pattern or "nervous water" on the surface can indicate larger schools of redfish. It is not unusual for schools of 50 or more redfish in the 6- to 10-pound class to move out of the deeper channels and waters of nearby Redfish Bay to feed in the shallows around Stedman.

The Stedman Island flats can be accessed by boat from public launch ramps at Aransas Pass or at the Fin and Feather Marina, which offers half-day and full-day skiff rentals.

Hog Island, also located on Redfish Bay, is another good site that is accessible by boat from public launch ramps and marinas at Aransas Pass and Port Aransas. Around the shoreline are deep holes that collect gamefish

This hard-fighting black drum took a crab fly near Rockport.

during low tides. Look for redfish around the shallow edges and for trout in deeper holes.

The *South Bay flats* are located across the Aransas Shrimp Boat Channel from the causeway road that links Aransas Pass with the ferry landing on Harbor Island. The nearest boat access to this area is available from marinas along the causeway and from the public launch ramps at Port Aransas and Aransas Pass. Kayakers frequently paddle across the channel to fish South Bay's expansive flats.

The expansive *Brown and Root flats* are known for holding schools of redfish. They also attract solitary female trout in the 25- to 30-inch range on occasion, says Corpus Christi fly-fishing guide Joe Mendez. The flats are marked by oyster reefs and by occasional soft bottoms on the north end. The south end has a mostly hard sand bottom that is excellent for wading and sightcasting. Tidal movements and changing water levels dictate whether anglers can enter the area by boat. If the tides are uncooperative, the site can be accessed on foot across a marshy shallows, from drive-up locations on Harbor Island, along the causeway road near the Port Aransas ferry landing. Only shallow-running skiffs or tunnel-drive boats should attempt to enter the flats even when tides are running high.

Corpus Christi Ship Channel

The *Corpus Christi ship channel* can be accessed on foot via the spoil island at the south end of the Brown and Root flats. It offers a good, hard bottom that allows wading to the edge of the channel drop-off, for casting to trout in the deeper water. Flyfishers who make the run down the Corpus Christi channel by boat can fish either side of the channel edges or access the Brown and Root flats by walking across the spoil island on the north shoreline.

The narrow strip of spoil islands directly across the Intracoastal Waterway from Conn Brown Harbor in Aransas Pass is an excellent site to prospect for trout and redfish. Redfish hold on the flats side, and schools of seatrout cruise and feed along the channel side near the drop-off. Flyfishers can wade to the edge of the channel and use Clouser Deep Minnow patterns to locate schools of trout in the deeper water. These spoil islands are accessible by boat from nearby marinas at Aransas Pass and on the causeway road (Texas 361), along the Aransas Shrimp Boat Channel.

Nearby is the *Morris and Cummings Cut,* a small boat channel that connects the Aransas Shrimp Boat Channel with Redfish Bay. Morris and Cummings attracts good numbers of redfish during the winter months. It can also fill up with fish in the summer during strong low-tide phases. Flyfishers should wade the edges or drift through it, casting uniform-density lines along the drop-off. The cut is accessible by boat from marinas on the causeway road at Aransas Pass (Texas 361).

Just southeast of Stedman Island, near the causeway road and accessible by skiff from several area marinas, is a very large grass flat that lies between Pelican Island and the end of Mustang Island. During periods of strong water movement, large trout will move up on it and face into the current to ambush baitfish, making this an ideal area to driftfish from a boat.

The nearby *East Flats,* an expansive, shallow estuary, is an excellent wadefishing and driftfishing area. Water depth on the flats varies from about 10 inches to 4 feet at a drop-off on the edge of Corpus Christi Bay. Sloughs, shorelines, and flats are marked with thick grass bottoms, potholes, and occasional scattered shell. The East Flats draw good numbers of redfish as well as big trout. Look for single redfish cruising and feeding with backs out of the water on shallower flats, and for groups of tailing fish feeding together in compact pods or "piles." This area of flats can be reached by boat from marinas and launch ramps at Port Aransas and Aransas Pass. It lies just south of the Corpus Christi channel, near the Mustang Island shoreline.

Catfish Flat, a wide stretch of light sand bottom marked by several duck blinds on the eastern edge of Redfish Bay, offers excellent sightcasting on an outgoing tide. With the sun at your back, you can see pods of red-fish from a distance as they move across the flat into the current. When they are feeding across this flat, they will sweep up anything in their path, including poppers and mud minnow and shrimp patterns.

Lydia Ann Channel Shorelines

The *Lydia Ann Channel* begins at Port Aransas, at the convergence of the Corpus Christi ship channel and Aransas Channel, and runs northeast be-tween Harbor and San Jose islands. Jack crevalle, ladyfish, and Spanish mackerel often school along the points at the entrance to the Lydia Ann. Schools of redfish frequently can be found feeding near the shorelines, and the channel edges attract gangs of school trout.

REDFISH BAY
(See map on page 88.)

Dagger Island on Redfish Bay is a good area to driftfish from a boat. Cast-ing over grass beds, look for fish around potholes and light sand patches. Dagger is known for holding clear water. When the tide drops out, it can be difficult to get even a shallow-draft boat in, but this is a good time to anchor in deeper water and walk in. The island is accessible from a num-ber of marinas and public ramps at Aransas Pass and Port Aransas. *Ran-som Island,* located north of the Corpus Christi ship channel, also is known for holding good numbers of trout and redfish. Both Dagger and Ransom islands are excellent areas for redfish on the "outside" in deeper water and on the "inside" along shallow flats. Ransom Island is also accessible by boat from marinas at Aransas Pass and Port Aransas.

MUSTANG ISLAND/CORPUS CHRISTI BAY
(See map on page 93.)

Wilson's Cut, a launch ramp and boat channel located south of Port Aransas off Texas 361 (across the road from the Sandpiper and Seagull Condominiums), offers access by boat to prime grass flats behind Sham-rock Island and Shamrock Cove. This is an excellent drive-up, walk-in wadefishing area where flyfishers have a chance of seeing good numbers of tailing redfish and black drum as well as getting an occasional shot at a solitary, heavyweight female speckled trout. The features present in the Wilson's Cut area—expansive flats with creeks and depressions—are ideal habitat for redfish and black drum. Flyfishers also can target school trout and flounder around the creek mouths.

  Kate's Hole, another fish-holding feature behind Mustang Island, draws commercial trotlining activity for black drum. It also is a good area

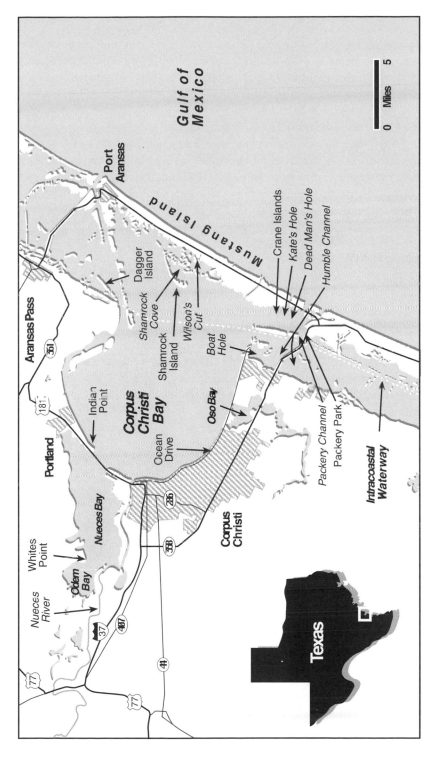

Gulf of Mexico

Port Aransas

Mustang Island

Crane Islands

Kate's Hole

Dead Man's Hole

Humble Channel

Aransas Pass

361

Dagger Island

Shamrock Cove

Shamrock Island

Wilson's Cut

Boat Hole

181

Indian Point

Corpus Christi Bay

Oso Bay

Ocean Drive

Packery Channel

Packery Park

Portland

286

Intracoastal Waterway

Nueces Bay

Corpus Christi

358

Whites Point

Odem Bay

361

Nueces River

37

181

44

77

77

Texas

0   Miles   5

93

for sightcasting because it holds clear water. The flats and spoil islands in the area between Kate's Hole and Deadman's Hole are good sites for wade-fishing and sightcasting during the summer months. It is located on Mustang Island shoreline just north of the JFK Causeway (Texas 22), southeast of Corpus Christi.

The grass flats and hard sand bottoms on the inside of the *Crane Islands* draw tailing redfish, especially in the morning. These flats are obscured from view from passing boat traffic on Corpus Christi Bay and offer flyfishers undisturbed waters for wadefishing and sightcasting. The Crane Islands area can be accessed by boat from marinas near the JFK Bridge in Corpus Christi, or by vehicle from a wellpad road off of Texas 361.

NUECES BAY AREA
(See map on page 93.)

Houston flyfisher Mark Lucas, who grew up fishing the shorelines around Odem Bay, Nueces Bay, Portland, and Ingleside, says the shallow oyster reefs around the high bridge that separates Corpus Christi Bay and Nueces Bay are heavily traveled by redfish and seatrout.

Nueces Bay offers flyfishers an area that is not heavily fished, says guide Joe Mendez of Corpus Christi. "If you find a place that is full of fish and there are fifty boats hammering it every day, that is one thing. But if you find a spot with nobody else, you don't need a huge amount of fish to catch a lot of fish."

Portland Area
Corpus Christi Bay offers excellent wadefishing in front of the Portland community, in the area around *Indian Point*. The site is accessible by car or on foot. Flyfishers can also launch a kayak at the Indian Point Pier to fish the point and a nearby oyster reef.

Toward the middle of Nueces Bay, the bottom gets boggy in about 2 to 4 feet of water. Fish-holding features here include oyster reefs, mud bottoms, and cordgrass shorelines. Redfish and trout hold along the reefs, and it is possible to find tailing fish near the grass along the shorelines.

Not many people wade the Portland shoreline, but 8- and 9-pound trout have been caught in that area over the years, says Portland native Mark Lucas. He recommends fishing the edge of the spoil island as well as sandbars and guts just off the 40-foot-deep Reynolds Channel. In this area, tailing reds often get back on the mud bottom flats around *Whites Point*. The area is not heavily fished because it is hard to reach and has soft bottoms in places. You can access it on the north shoreline from Odem via Farm Roads 893 and 1074.

Odem Bay, behind Whites Point off Nueces Bay, includes a large marsh with a number of tidal creeks. It is shallow and hard to reach by boat but ideal for a sea kayak. Odem Bay is a prolific shrimp nursery benefitting from the fresh water released upstream from Lake Corpus Christi and the Nueces River (see map on page 93). Redfish, trout, black drum, and flounder are found in these bays. Look for birds working over trout in the spring. Reef fishing in the area also is productive. A steady southeast wind over 10 mph will muddy up the water in Odem Bay, but the estuary is productive during the winter months and can be fished effectively in a north wind.

The shallow waters around the Portland–Corpus Christi causeway, where the Corpus Christi and Nueces bays meet are known to hold good numbers of trout and redfish. The area has many features attractive to fish, including a big oyster field, guts, and smaller oyster bars. When the tide comes in, it flushes over these bars, and fish hold behind the reefs. A peak fishing period here is in the spring, when the shrimp start migrating and you can find trout and redfish feeding actively. The bay also provides good fishing in late fall and winter. Periods of heavy freshwater runoff or upstream releases on Nueces and Odem bays can adversely affect fishing until these systems balance out. Local anglers say wadefishing can be good along Corpus Christi's scenic *Ocean Drive.*

Nearby *Oso Bay* also offers productive wadefishing and is a good area for fishing out of a kayak. Oso Bay receives a warm-water discharge that is from the CP&L power plant, and redfish stack up there in the winter months.

The *Humble Channel* and the *Boat Hole* on the north end of the Laguna Madre hold trout and redfish in water 2 to 3 feet deep. There are a number of wadable flats in the area. Large schools of redfish stage in this area during the summer and fall months.

Another productive fly-fishing destination in the Corpus Christi area is *Packery Channel and Park.* The channel offers drive-up, walk-in wade fishing. Flyfishers can launch a kayak here to fish the far shoreline. At dawn, redfish move up into the channel shallows to chase baitfish. The park is located on Texas 22 (South Padre Island Drive), east of the JFK Causeway Bridge near the Texas 361 turnoff to Port Aransas.

UPPER LAGUNA MADRE (EAST SHORELINE)
(See map on page 97.)

Night Hawk Bay is a shallow estuary located near a residential development between the north end of Padre Island and the Intracoastal Waterway. The Night Hawk flats offer excellent wadefishing and sightcasting prospects over hard sand bottoms, grass beds, and potholes. Some parts of this flat are inaccessible except for walk-in wading and sea kayaks. The small, narrow bay is located between the east shore of the Laguna Madre and a spoil island that runs along the Intracoastal Waterway. It runs for 8 miles from the Padre Isles subdivision to Bird Island Basin.

The launch ramp at *Bird Island Basin,* near Corpus Christi, provides a jumping-off point to prime upper Laguna Madre flats and shorelines from Baffin Bay to the Kennedy Land Cut and the Graveyard (see Chapter 6). Excellent wadefishing also is available just a short walk from the boat launch. Take the path along the cordgrass to get around the small basin on the north side of the launch ramp. After walking a short distance on the island, anglers can reenter the water and work the shoreline and flats to the north. By walking north, flyfishers can avoid the boat traffic and windsurfing activities that usually take place to the south. Flyfishers can work the shore for tailing redfish early and late in the day or wade the hard sand bottoms and grass flats around the nearby spoil islands for speckled trout and flounder. There is a lot of surface baitfish activity on these flats, and small poppers and finger-mullet patterns are good choices to work on or near the top. Bird Island Basin is located inside the Padre Island National Seashore, an 80-mile-long, virtually undeveloped segment of the barrier island that begins just below Corpus Christi. The Padre Island National Seashore is 12 miles south of the JFK Bridge in Corpus Christi. Take Park Road 22 to the Seashore entrance. A $10 entry fee per vehicle is good for seven days' admittance to the Seashore, and an annual pass is $20. Parking at the Bird Island Basin launch ramp area is $5 per day per vehicle or $10 for an annual pass.

UPPER LAGUNA MADRE (WEST SHORELINE)
(See map on page 97.)

Located on the western shore of the upper Laguna Madre, the *King Ranch shoreline* is a productive area for reds and trout and an excellent choice for fly fishing. The site draws a lot of boats but can offer excellent wadefishing in light to moderate wind conditions. When the wind kicks up, making the water murky along the shoreline, there are opportunities for flyfishers casting shooting heads from a drifting boat in water 4 to 6 feet deep. Drift anchors are often necessary to slow down drifting boats in the stiff winds but anglers can cover lots of water this way and have a chance at trout, reds, and black drum. "Whenever you have a strong wind, you want to go to a big body of water," says Corpus Christi fly-fishing guide Joe Mendez. "It feels like you are catching a lot of fish, but it is because you are covering a lot of water. If you go back on a calm day, you may not catch anything because

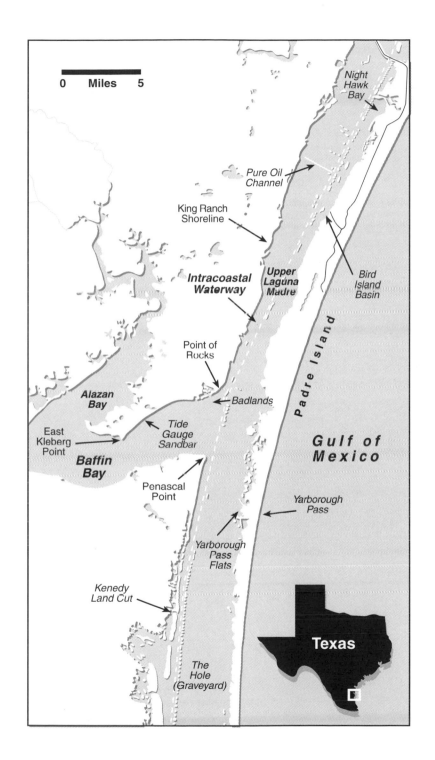

0   Miles   5

Night
Hawk
Bay

Pure Oil
Channel

King Ranch
Shoreline

*Intracoastal
Waterway*

**Upper
Laguna
Madre**

Bird
Island
Basin

Padre Island

Point of
Rocks

*Alazan
Bay*

Badlands

East
Kleberg
Point

*Tide
Gauge
Sandbar*

**Gulf of
Mexico**

**Baffin
Bay**

Penascal
Point

Yarborough
Pass

Yarborough
Pass
Flats

Kenedy
Land Cut

Texas

The
Hole
(Graveyard)

you are not covering the water." On the other hand, Mendez says, calm conditions are ideal for driftfishing smaller areas around spoil islands. "That is when you want a lighter wind, so you will stay in the zone longer."

The *Pure Oil Channel*, which bisects the King Ranch shoreline, attracts good numbers of redfish, trout, and black drum. Anglers can access this site by boat from marinas around the JFK Bridge at Corpus Christi. Flyfishers will have success drifting across the channel or anchoring up and casting along the channel edges.

CHAPTER SIX

LOWER COAST FLATS

BAFFIN BAY TO BROWNSVILLE

Angler's Log
East Cut, Port Mansfield
July 1996

We were wading in eight to ten inches of water over a grass-and-sand bottom. We had been fishing the area for about two weeks and it had been holding a lot of fish. One day there would be redfish and the next day there would be trout, back and forth.

This one day, though, the trout were just cruising along under the redfish, in their shadow almost. You would see one to three trout following them. The trick was to get the fly in a position close enough to the trout so you didn't catch the redfish. That made it exciting.

Capt. Terry Neal, Port Mansfield

In contrast to the closed bays, remote barrier island tidal lakes, and oyster reefs that characterize the middle stretch of the coast from Port O'Connor to Corpus Christi, the lower Texas coast is dominated by a long, open, river-like estuary called the Laguna Madre, which is shielded from the Gulf of Mexico by Padre Island, the world's longest barrier island. One of the chief characteristics that sets this area apart from the upper and middle coasts is that much of the lower coast lies along privately owned ranchlands, requiring anglers to travel substantial distances by flats boats to reach productive flats and shorelines. Many guides and recreational boaters, especially those traveling south from Corpus Christi, think nothing of making round-trips of 60 to 70 miles daily just to reach prime flats. With an average depth of 2.5 feet, the Laguna Madre's sand-and-grass flats are a flyfisher's dream. Shallow-running flats boats, some equipped with towers and poling platforms to provide a better vantage point for locating fish on the expansive flats, are a favorite among guides and recreational anglers on this part of the coast.

From its northern end at the JFK Bridge in Corpus Christi, the Laguna Madre runs southward for 100 miles to the resort community of South Padre Island, near the Mexican border. At South Padre Island, the Laguna Madre converges just above the Rio Grande with a pass to the Gulf. The pass is close to a small, enclosed estuary and a deepwater ship channel that provide a variety of gamefish habitats. Other important angling features along this upper stretch of coast include the King Ranch shoreline, Baffin Bay, Graveyard, and Kenedy Land Cut.

The Laguna Madre plays a vital role as a nursery for a variety of gamefish. It is famous for the size and abundance of its seatrout as well as for holding large herds of redfish. The lower coast fishery, supported by the Laguna Madre estuary, has thrived despite devastating freezes in 1983 and 1989 and more recent bouts with a nontoxic but water-staining algal bloom known as "brown tide."

Access to the upper end of the Laguna Madre and Baffin Bay is from marinas and boat ramps near Corpus Christi or at Bird Island Basin, a recreational area on the Padre Island National Seashore. Flyfishers also can access the Laguna Madre flats from marinas and public launch ramps at Port Mansfield and Arroyo City.

The waters around Port Mansfield, located off Texas 186, 26 miles east of Raymondville, have been a favorite for light-tackle anglers for a half century. Port Mansfield offers visiting flyfishers motels and condos, launch ramps and marinas, as well as broad, sandy flats, jetty fishing, and a nearby pass to the Gulf.

There also are motels and marinas at nearby Port Isabel and South Padre Island. The venerable Port Isabel Yacht Club, founded in 1926, still rents rooms to visiting anglers and offers an excellent restaurant and bar.

A wide range of fly patterns and colors—from buggy shrimp imitations to Crazy Charlie bonefish flies—are effective on the flats of the lower coast. See pages 24–27 in chapter 3 for more information on fly patterns.

BAFFIN BAY AREA
(See map on page 97.)

Baffin Bay is a 25-mile run by boat from the marinas around the JFK Causeway Bridge at Corpus Christi. Famous for its big trout, Baffin Bay has been difficult for anglers using flies and other artificials in recent years because of the effect of the "brown tide" algal bloom on water clarity. However, there are encouraging signs that the algae are receding and clear water is returning on a number of Baffin Bay flats and shorelines. "If you have water clarity, the fly fishing is excellent around the rocks in Baffin," says guide Joe Mendez, referring to the prehistoric rock formations created by colonies of serpulid worms. Unique to Baffin Bay, these large "rocks" lie just under the surface in many instances and require boaters to be extremely cautious when navigating these waters.

One of the many Baffin Bay features that hold trout and redfish is the shallow flat that runs along the *Tide Gauge* sandbar. Boaters can access this area by boat, heading south along the King Ranch shoreline. A right turn at the Point of Rocks at the opening to Baffin Bay and crossing an area called Cat Head, where state record–setting spotted seatrout have been caught, brings you to Tide Gauge, a long, light sandbar that runs all the way to East Kleberg Point. Here waders will find water clear enough to fish even when the brown tide is present. Tailing redfish also show up on this feature. Fly-fishing guide Joe Mendez recommends medium-sized lead-eyed Clousers or large poppers around the edges of the rocks. The Red Minnow pattern, a fly tied by Buddy Weir and described as "a cross between a Deceiver and Keys tarpon fly," also has worked well in the Baffin area on reds and trout.

Yarborough Pass/Yarborough Pass Flats

Just south of the mouth of Baffin Bay on the barrier island side of the Laguna Madre are *Yarborough Pass* and *Yarborough Pass Flats*. These sites can be reached by water or land vehicle via the Padre Island National Seashore. Yarborough Pass is located at the 15-mile marker, about midway between Big Shell and Little Shell beaches on the Seashore. Once a link between the Laguna Madre and the Gulf of Mexico, the pass was long ago sealed off by wave action and shifting sands. Today it provides an access point to miles of ankle- to knee-deep wadefishing on the upper Laguna Madre.

A four-wheel-drive vehicle is essential to navigate the short stretch of soft sand on the fore-island dune ridge. Once you're over the hump, it's an easy run of about a mile over a hard sand surface to the lagoon. Some anglers trailer in their shallow-draft boats and launch from the old dock at Yarborough Pass. This provides access to prime fishing on the nearby flats as well as Baffin Bay, the Kenedy Land Cut, and the Graveyard.

About 35 miles down from the JFK Bridge is the *Kenedy Land Cut.* This narrow, 22-mile stretch of the Laguna Madre lined with fishing shacks and floating houseboats holds trout and redfish in its deep channel as well as along its shallow, light sand shorelines. Flyfishers who make the trip often will find schools of seatrout chasing shrimp on the surface in the middle of the channel. Look for diving birds as a sign that trout are feeding in the area. Flycasters fishing from skiffs with trolling motors have miles of sightcasting opportunities for tailing and cruising trout and redfish that move up on the grass beds and light sand bottoms along the shoreline. Since the wind normally is blowing out of the southeast, the west side of the cut is the most favorable for flycasting. Look for trout and reds tailing or following stingrays along the dark grass beds at the edge of the channel drop-off and near depressions at creek mouths.

Another intriguing lower coastal feature in this area is the *Graveyard*. The Graveyard, or Nine-Mile Hole, is a broad, shallow tidal flat accessed by several channels on the east side of the Kenedy Land Cut. During the late spring and summer months it can draw large schools of redfish as well as large trout, black drum, and ladyfish. The bottom varies from firm to boggy. It is a prime area for driftfishing, wading, and sightcasting, but knowledge of tidal movements in the area and a shallow-draft boat are required, to avoid ending up high and dry. Corpus Christi fly-fishing guides Joe Mendez and Bill Sheka, Jr. regularly track redfish schools in the Graveyard.

PORT MANSFIELD AREA

Continuing south, anglers enter the waters around Port Mansfield, the heart of the lower Laguna Madre. Just south of the Kenedy Land Cut is *Gladis' Hole*, a broad, grass flat where redfish that are moving south from the Land Cut and the Graveyard sometimes gang up. This is a good area in which to driftfish from a boat. It often holds clear water and can be ideal for sightcasting to trout as well as reds.

Some of the best fly-fishing features on the lower Laguna Madre are located within sight of the Port Mansfield water tower along the *East Cut*, a channel that connects the port to the jettied pass at the Gulf. Deepwater drop-offs, narrow channels, spoil island shorelines, and broad flats with firm white sand bottoms and thick grass beds are among the East Cut features that attract and hold trout, redfish, flounder, and ladyfish. Veteran Port Mansfield fly-fishing guide Terry Neal says the most favorable water movement occurs on the north side of the East Cut. "You have your fresh Gulf water coming in (from the pass) and the fish migrate in," he says. "Schools of redfish come in here and go both ways when they come into the bay." Neal says drive-up wadefishing is limited out of Port Mansfield, but under favorable weather conditions you can reach prime East Cut spoil islands and flats in a flat-bottomed johnboat with a 15-hp motor.

The shallow flats north of Marker 17, described locally as "north of the East Cut," offer firm sand bottoms and grass beds. This area is known to hold good numbers of redfish and is ideal for wadefishing and sightcasting. There are also good shoreline features around the old King Ranch fence and pier.

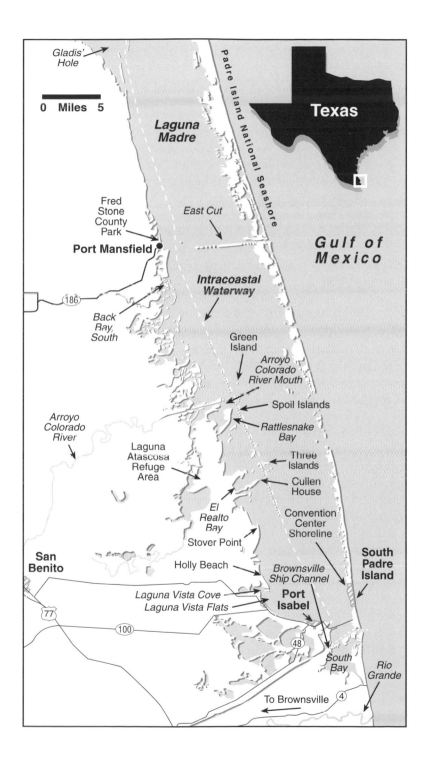

Gladis'
Hole

0 Miles 5

*Laguna
Madre*

Padre Island National Seashore

Texas

Fred
Stone
County
Park

East Cut

Port Mansfield

Gulf of
Mexico

186

*Intracoastal
Waterway*

*Back
Bay,
South*

Green
Island

*Arroyo
Colorado
River Mouth*

*Arroyo
Colorado
River*

Spoil Islands

Laguna
Atascosa
Refuge
Area

*Rattlesnake
Bay*

Three
Islands

Cullen
House

*El
Realto
Bay*

Convention
Center
Shoreline

Stover Point

**South
Padre
Island**

**San
Benito**

Holly Beach

*Brownsville
Ship Channel*

Laguna Vista Cove

**Port
Isabel**

Laguna Vista Flats

77

100

48

*South
Bay*

*Rio
Grande*

To Brownsville

4

Fred Stone County Park in Port Mansfield offers drive-up, walk-in wadefishing. While many waders will walk out to fish in waist-deep water, local guides like Neal advise flyfishers to stay in shallower water close to the shore because redfish will move up near the bank to chase baitfish. There are other good areas farther up the shoreline, but a boat is required to access them.

Traveling south from Port Mansfield by boat, just off the Intracoastal Waterway near the west shoreline of the Laguna Madre lie a series of sunken spoil islands. Created by dredging activity in the Intracoastal Waterway, all are within 6 miles of Port Mansfield. Whenever the water is down, some of these islands are exposed. Redfish and large trout will move up into the shallows and tail around the edges of these islands, Neal says. He recommends wadefishers look here for gamefish. Fish will also move up into the grass beds. "I have kicked up big, big trout and redfish around these features," Neal says.

Located next to the north end of the Laguna Atascosa Wildlife Refuge is an estuary called *Back Bay, South*. This remote, backcountry lagoon lies in what was the old Arroyo Colorado riverbed. Boat access is limited to the mouth of this estuary, even with shallow-running flats skiffs. This soft-bottomed marshy flat is ideal for fly fishing from a sea kayak. "Some of the biggest trout in the whole laguna live in here in numbers," says fly-fishing guide Terry Neal. "It is a sanctuary for fish."

ARROYO COLORADO RIVER AREA

Proceeding south from Port Mansfield, boaters will find a variety of excellent flats and spoil islands to fish around the mouth of the Arroyo Colorado River. The spoil islands east of the Arroyo offer excellent sightcasting prospects, but poling or driftfishing is required because of soft bottoms.

Green Island is located in this area. The flat running east of this island is one of the favorite wadefishing and sightcasting destinations for lower Laguna Madre flyfishers. Features include hard sand and grass bottoms with potholes. Trout frequently will stack up around cuts where there is water movement. And don't be surprised on occasion to find that a fly thrown into a pod of tailing redfish sometimes gets pounced on first by a big trout.

Rattlesnake Bay is another prime angling destination located near the mouth of the Arroyo Colorado. Its shorelines and spoil islands are known to hold large trout. Flyfishers should focus on the area behind the spoil islands. A nearby slough, which holds trout and tailing redfish, has a soft bottom but is ideal for fishing from a kayak. This bay is seldom fished because it is such a small system. But the cuts that come off the old well channels, marked by wellheads on local fishing maps, provide habitat for trout and redfish. Fish congregate in those old silted-in channels even if there is only a 6-inch difference in water depth between the channel and an adjacent flat. Flyfishers should target these features on days when the water clears in these cuts and you can pole down the middle of the channel looking for targets. The old pipelines also have pothole-like indentions that often hold fish. These deepwater features are best fished on low tides. When tides start coming back in, the fish will move out of the channels, and it is wise for anglers to fish the edges of the drop-offs and back on the flats.

The spoil islands along the east and west sides of the Intracoastal Waterway on this part of the Laguna Madre (from Port Mansfield south to below the mouth of the Arroyo Colorado River) regularly attract and hold some of the highest concentrations of big sow trout on the lower coast. From early summer through August, look for trout and occasionally redfish feeding over stingrays around spoil islands. Some of these spoil islands are wadable. Others have soft bottoms that require flyfishers to drift or pole across in a flats boat. Laguna Madre guide Eric Glass says uniform-density or sink-tip lines with Clouser Minnow patterns can produce exciting trout action here during the summer months.

Three Islands Area

The flats on the east side of *Three Islands* near the old houseboats provide excellent wadefishing and sightcasting options for waders. The expansive flats extend to the east shoreline of the Laguna. Water levels can vary from a few inches to waist deep along light sand and grass beds. It is about a 45-minute run by flats boat from Port Mansfield to these flats. The resort condos on South Padre Island are visible to the south. This is a prime sightcasting area where flyfishers often will find reds, trout, and ladyfish cruising and feeding together. The most productive areas are the edges where grass beds meet the light sand bottoms.

From the Cullen House to Stover Point

Cullen Bay, a small bay system located near the *Cullen House,* a private residence and local landmark, offers an attractive mix of flats and shoreline features that draw trout and redfish on moving tides. The area can be adversely affected by boat traffic, but there are a number of more remote flats nearby that will draw fish on a high tide. Waders should move in with the incoming tide to the shallowest areas and then move out with the retreating tide. The shoreline from the Cullen House to Stover Point has many small islands with sandbars, patches of grass, and light sand bottoms. The

Casting for redfish, trout, and snook in the Brownsville Ship Channel.

area can attract single tailing redfish and pods of tailing fish as well as groups of ten or more cruising fish.

The tidal lakes in the vicinity of nearby *El Realto Bay* are excellent for redfish during high-tide periods, especially in the late summer and fall.

Another intriguing feature on this lower end of the Laguna Madre is *Unnecessary Island*. Once exposed and visible, Unnecessary Island is now a subsurface high spot with a sand-and-shell bottom where big sow trout are known to hang out. An old gas well channel dead-ends at this feature, and large trout tend to move up on the high spot. The area is wadable but most often is fished from a drifting boat with towers for spotting trout. Unnecessary Island is located roughly on a line drawn between the southernmost spoil island on the west side of the Laguna Madre below the Arroyo Colorado mouth, and the Cullen House. If you can find the island, you might get a chance at big trout and redfish, local guides say.

SOUTH PADRE ISLAND/PORT ISABEL AREA
(See map on page 103.)

This prolific fishery on the lower Laguna Madre near the border with Mexico is the northernmost range for snook on the Texas coast. Thanks in part to a series of mild winters, reduced size and bag limits, and favorable habitat, anglers have enjoyed a marked resurgence in snook fishing in these waters in recent seasons. The oyster reefs and mangrove shorelines of South

Angler Eric Glass fights a 10-pound snook at South Padre Island.

Bay, the creek mouths, and the rocky shorelines along the Brownsville Ship Channel and Laguna Madre bridge structure provide prime habitat for snook and are easily accessible from area launch ramps.

In recent years, the Texas Parks and Wildlife Department has reduced the daily bag limit on snook to one fish per day with a slot limit of 24 to 28 inches. However, the narrow range and fragile nature of this great gamefish in Texas waters has prompted most anglers to voluntarily release their catch.

In the Brownsville Ship Channel, flyfishers can cast for snook and snappers under and around oil service and grain-loading docks while mariachi music serenades them from anchored shrimp boats. At the next stop at South Bay, anglers can sightcast over secluded grass flats where the only sound is the soft rustle of wings as roseate spoonbills and reddish egrets flutter along the mangrove shorelines. And just a short run north to the Laguna Atascosa Refuge shoreline, anglers have a good chance of finding redfish cruising over light-sand bottoms.

In addition to snook, the grass flats and shorelines of the Lower Laguna Madre hold big numbers of redfish and seatrout. On these broad, open flats, anglers often find ladyfish and black drum on the prowl for food alongside the redfish and trout. The nearby jetties at Brazos Santiago Pass attract tarpon in the summer and early fall—15- to 35-pounders that can be found in the late afternoon rolling and chasing bait schools at the edges of the rocks.

Flyfishers have a chance to cast at big schools of redfish that hang around the open flats of the lower Laguna during the late summer months, as they begin staging for their migration out the nearby pass in the fall. Flyfishers casting to these schools that can number two hundred fish or more should use floating lines and flies that will sink rapidly, such as bendbacks or Clouser Deep Minnow patterns. Fish in these large schools are moving more quickly than it appears, and weighted flies will get down to their eye level rapidly, whereas heavily hackled flies will lie on the surface while a hundred redfish swim under them.

South Padre Island Shoreline

The shoreline in this area is marked by a broad sandbar rimmed by a grass flat and includes a series of deep troughs, features that now draw redfish and trout. The site is a short run by boat from South Padre marinas. Wadefishers can drive up the beach and walk onto the flats in the vicinity of the second county building on South Padre Island Beach. Boaters and drive-up waders have easy access to the shoreline in front of the South Padre Island Convention Center. Flyfishers can enter the flats from the walkway and nature trail on the south side of the convention center. There is a deep hole near the shore that draws speckled trout. The best time to fish this flat is the early morning.

Almost in the shadow of the South Padre condominiums, near the end of the bridge on South Padre Island, is a mangrove shoreline. This stretch of shoreline, between the causeway bridge and the Texas Parks and Wildlife–operated public boat launch, offers drive-up, walk-in access and a chance at trout, redfish, and snook. Look for baitfish activity around coves and shell bars, and fish the incoming and outgoing tides early and late.

Laguna Atascosa Refuge Area

The Laguna Atascosa Refuge is located about 6 miles north of Port Isabel and can be reached by road or by water. For boaters, Port Isabel guide Gilbert Vela recommends working the spoil banks and the shorelines along the refuge shorelines. "There are no oysters out there so you look for humps, little sandbars, and drop-offs," he says. The refuge is open to visitors, but walk-in wadefishing is not allowed from refuge property. It can be productive, however, especially during the spring months, to go to the refuge and drive down the bayfront road on the evening before a fishing trip, to look for birds working over tailing fish. With a 20-minute drive from Port Isabel, you can locate fish and save on-the-water running time the next day. A good pair of binoculars is a worthwhile accessory on these scouting trips.

The nearby *Laguna Vista* cove and flats attract considerable walk-in wadefishing during the summer and are also an excellent winter fishery. Another location famous for holding large trout is *Holly Beach*. Boat traffic is usually light in this area because of its proximity to Port Isabel and its attraction for walk-in wadefishers. There are lightly fished spoil islands accessible by boat on the outside of this shoreline, and nearby, deeper flats that regularly hold trout and redfish.

South Bay

South Bay is a pristine mangrove-lined estuary located within a 20-minute run by flats boat from launch ramps and marinas on South Padre and Port Isabel. The bay system with its many small creeks offers sightcasting over secluded grass flats. South Bay also is a must stop for South Padre's top snook guides: Gilbert Vela, Gib Little, and Eric Glass look for snook along the estuary's mangrove shorelines and scattered oyster bars. Tide levels are critical in the bay, Vela says. He says spring tides and high water from tropical depressions often set off snook action. When there is good tidal movement, flyfishers should look for redfish, trout, flounder, and snook tight to the shorelines or stationed at ambush points on the edges of tidal creeks.

Brownsville Ship Channel

Sixteen miles long and 38 feet deep, the Brownsville ship channel provides a year-around haven for fish. For a variety of gamefish, the channel is both a river link to the Gulf of Mexico and an inshore reef providing a deep-water sanctuary and a rich food supply. In addition to being one of the best snook fisheries on the coast, the channel is home to red drum, spotted seatrout, ladyfish, jack crevalle, flounder, and black drum and will have occasional shows of juvenile tarpon. There also has been a noticeable increase in recent years in the numbers of gray or mangrove snapper in the channel. The species is attracted to the rocky structure found in many places along the channel's edges.

The summer months are prime times to fish the ship channel from a boat, casting Clouser, Whistler, and Deceiver patterns up against the shoreline and creek mouths for trout, redfish, and snook. Guides Gilbert Vela and Eric Glass target snook around little creeks and shoreline structure of the ship channel as well as along the drop-off. "If you see them working, you approach as cautiously as you can," Vela says. "You know you will get at least one hit from a snook, and you might get a red or a trout." Flyfishers should look for snook popping and slapping the water as they attack baitfish massing around the edges of feeder creeks emptying into the channel.

The Brownsville Ship Channel can be accessed from the Texas Parks and Wildlife Department launch ramp on San Martin Lake, located on Texas 48 between Port Isabel and Brownsville.

CHAPTER SEVEN

FLY FISHING BY NIGHT

Angler's Log
Brownsville Ship Channel at Old Coast Guard Dock
August 1989

We had been watching that snook sitting there motionless. I could see him under the lights. I was using a number six saltwater Zonker pattern, and I threw at him and threw at him. Finally, I made a cast in the lights and he started tracking that little tiny Zonker, just waddling behind it all the way to the boat, and then, poom!—I caught it on a 9-weight, and the fight wasn't long. When they are that close to an obstruction, you tighten up on them and see what breaks first. We landed it, measured it and released it. The fish was 34 inches, about 12 or 13 pounds.

Capt. Eric Glass, South Padre Island

t is around 3 A.M., and the lighted pier near the Rockport Harbor is deserted. A flyfisher walks out carefully onto the dark pier, knowing that one heavy-footed step can shake the rickety boards and pilings all the way to the end, sending out vibrations that will spook any big trout in the neighborhood.

Shielded by the darkness, the flyfisher freezes when he sees, just ahead in the clear water under a bank of lights, the long shadow of a trout in the 30-inch class. In the early morning stillness, this big female had moved out of the safety of the nearby channel to look for an easy meal under the lights. Knowing that he will probably get only one cast at this fish, the angler lays the little Deceiver down softly in the darkness, just beyond the lighted circle on the water. The fly glides untouched through the ring of light, and the outline of the trout fades into the darkness. The flyfisher feels disappointment but also a measure of satisfaction. After all, every time an angler gets the chance to go one-on-one with a monster trout, a valuable lesson is learned—and the next meeting might have a better ending.

Getting a shot with a fly and hooking a big trout haloed under the bright lights of a bayside pier doesn't happen very often. But anglers up and down the Texas coast are finding that a fly fished at night from lighted boat docks, piers, and jetties is one of the surest ways ever invented to catch school trout as well as ladyfish, redfish, snook, and flounder. A light focused on the water draws and concentrates swarms of baitfish and shrimp, and it doesn't take long for trout and other gamefish to take notice. The cafeteria-style offering is hard to resist.

On the Texas coast, you will know immediately if lighted water is productive by the "popping" sounds that trout make when they attack shrimp and minnows on the surface. When the action heats up, the night-feeding performance will include the flashes and boils of bigger fish, as well as iridescent white shrimp doing a life-and-death water ballet.

Frequently flies will "match the hatch" of small minnows in the water, often drawing more strikes than larger artificial lures and even live shrimp in these nighttime environments. The neutral density and slow sink rate of small glass minnow and shrimp patterns often give a fly a more natural look in the current, a big advantage under the lights.

Fly fishing at night from one of the many low-lying piers along the Texas coast offers a pleasant change from the physical and mental demands and advanced angling skills sometimes required for success in stalking redfish under a blistering sun or along a windswept shoreline. A lighted pier is a good place to introduce beginning flyfishers and young anglers to saltwater fly fishing. The odds of a successful outing are good, and a long, accurate cast is not necessary since the fish often are concentrated within a few feet of the pier. Having a pier all to yourself is the most desirable night-fishing option; but flyfishers can easily share space on the boards with the baitcasting and popping cork set. Look for a corner that allows room for an unobstructed backcast, or practice a compact roll cast.

Although the majority of fish attracted to the lights along the Texas coast are undersize seatrout in the 12- to 14-inch range that must be released, they can provide exciting action on light fly tackle. Fly rods matched to 5-weight lines can be used under light wind conditions. It is especially wise at night to bend down the barbs on hooks. This makes for solid hook-ups and quick and clean releases.

School trout on nighttime feeding binges can be oblivious to the hubbub that emanates from most crowded piers, but it is best to target larger fish in the early morning hours after the crowds have left. And although many low-lying bayside piers are ideal for fly fishing at night, the high piers

Night fishing at Aransas Pass, Phil Shook casts from a softly lit pier.

and crowded rails on the Gulf side of the barrier islands are best fished with conventional levelwind and spinning tackle.

After-hours fly fishing under the lights is equally exciting from a boat. Several Texas outfitters now offer overnight excursions behind the barrier islands on houseboats equipped with powerful lights for nighttime fishing. Anglers can cast flies around lighted docks or beachhouse piers. Enterprising flyfishers also can set up their own portable light systems along creek mouths or channel drop-offs. A full moon and a high tide are good conditions in which to target trout and reds, with or without lights.

In setting up lights at night, anglers should look for the same mix of features that attract gamefish during the day, including the presence of baitfish and strong water movement across channel edges, shell bars, grass flats, and tidal creeks.

TACKLE

Flies
A variety of fly patterns tied on #6 to #1 hooks that imitate or simulate shrimp and "glass minnows" are deadly under the lights. Chico's Bonefish Special and Clouser Deep Minnow patterns dressed with white, yellow, or

chartreuse deer hair and Krystal Flash are deadly under the lights for trout, redfish, and flounder.

Bendbacks with flashy wing material and dark-hackled SeaDucers also are proven producers at night.

POPULAR PIERS FOR NIGHTTIME FLY FISHING

For exciting nighttime fly fishing, look for the lights on the water or turn on your own. The following sites are among the most productive for nighttime fly fishing.

Upper Coast

Texas City Dike

Texas fly-fishing guide Dan Lynch says he uses a Par 64 Very Narrow Spot lighting system with 1,000-watt lamps to fly fish around the pilings and piers of the Texas City Dike. "Once the slack tide comes in, trout tend to go crazy for about an hour, and then they will quit," Lynch says. "Once the water starts moving again, they start doing their thing again." Lynch says he seeks areas where there are eddying currents. "This is where (the trout) will hold, in those pools, and let the bait come to them."

Lynch says he sets up his lights between the Texas City Dike fishing pier and the channel, where submerged pilings from an old pier create the eddying currents that make it a hotspot for redfish and trout.

Follets Island

The shoreline along the San Luis County Park (Old KOA Campground) on Follets Island is a popular summer night-fishing area on the upper coast. There is fixed lighting from several poles along the shoreline, and many anglers also set up their own systems. The shoreline is shallow and wadable, with a hard sand bottom. An effective strategy here is to wade out a short distance and cast to the far edges of the light beams.

Middle Coast

Matagorda

Trout, redfish, and sand trout move off the flats and concentrate in the deeper, warmer water of the Colorado River during the winter months. The Colorado, which intersects East Matagorda and West Matagorda bays, is an ideal winter night-fishing destination. Several motels and marinas including Allen's Landing, Carla Courts, River Bend Bait Camp, and Hageman's offer night fishing for a fee from lighted piers on the east bank of the Colorado River, near the town of Matagorda.

Matagorda is located about 100 miles south of Houston. From Houston take I-59 to Wharton. Turn left on Texas 60 and follow it to Matagorda.

Seadrift
Marinas and launch ramps on the Intracoastal Waterway near Seadrift are the staging areas for several outfitters who provide houseboat access to backcountry fishing behind Matagorda Island. The houseboats are equipped with light systems, and the nighttime fly fishing can be explosive during the summer and fall months along spoil islands and passes inside the barrier islands. Guide and outfitter Mark Koliba with Morningstar Boat Rental in Port O'Connor provides fishing and kayaking expeditions behind Matagorda Island that include nighttime fly fishing from a houseboat equipped with galley, head, and air-conditioned sleeping quarters.

Lamar Peninsula
The lighted fishing pier at Goose Island State Park, off Texas 35 and Park Road 13 north of Rockport, attracts trout and redfish on moving tides. Fly-fishers can cast from the pier or step off it and wade along the series of small spoil islands and cuts, casting back into the lights. There is a small fee for entering the park.

Fulton
Sportsman Manor in Fulton is among a number of motels that offer lighted piers for guests along Fulton Beach Road. This pier attracts large numbers of school trout at night during the summer months.

Rockport
Surf Court Motel and Laguna Reef Hotel in Rockport are two lodging facilities that have lighted fishing piers available for their guests. The Surf Court pier has the advantage, attracting larger trout from a nearby channel that leads into Rockport Harbor.

Aransas Pass
Fishing is allowed for a small fee off lighted piers operated by the Fin and Feather Marina and Bait Bucket Marina located on opposite sides of the Morris and Cummings Cut. These marinas are reachable via the causeway road between Aransas Pass and the Port Aransas ferry landing. At night, the piers here draw large numbers of school trout as well as redfish and flounder.

Angler Shawn Flanagan shows off the beauty of the speckled trout under the lights.

Port Aransas

The base of the south jetty at Port Aransas, near the University of Texas Marine Science Institute pier, is an excellent night-fishing destination during the summer and fall months. In addition to the jetty rocks and pier pilings, a submerged boxcar provides ideal habitat for a variety of gamefish including trout, redfish, and Spanish mackerel.

Since the jetty surface is irregular in this area, it is a good idea to scout it out during daylight hours and to plan night-fishing strategies in advance. Uniform-density lines or shooting tapers are recommended here because of the strong currents moving in and out of the pass. When the current is moving, when trout are busting and popping on the surface and white pelicans are herding baitfish in the light, the sights and sounds make this one of the most exciting night-fishing destinations on the coast. The trout run larger along this channel, and flyfishers are challenged to turn a fish before it can run into the pier pilings.

JFK Bridge Area, Corpus Christi

Several marinas along the upper Laguna Madre offer fishing from lighted piers for a small fee. One of these is Clem's, a marina and bait stand on the

Padre Island side of the JFK Bridge, below Corpus Christi. During periods when the current is moving, good numbers of trout will hold and feed in the lights around this pier. To get to Clem's, the only large pier that is lighted for night fishing, travel south from Corpus Christi. After crossing the JFK Bridge, take the first road to the right. Follow the road back under the bridge, bear left, and stop at the first bait stand on the right.

Lower Coast

Port Mansfield

Port Mansfield's harbor has many lighted boat slips and waterside condominiums with piers that offer excellent night-fishing opportunities during the summer and fall. Fly-fishing guests casting at night around the lighted boat slips at Sun Chase condos often take keeper trout and flounder.

South Padre Island

The channel running along the bay side of South Padre Island's resort community has a number of lighted docks, private homes, and marinas that draw schools of trout and ladyfish at night.

CHAPTER EIGHT

DECEIVERS IN THE ROCKS

FLY FISHING THE COASTAL JETTIES

Angler's Log
South Jetty, Port Mansfield
Summer 1991

The very end of the rocks on the south jetty at Port Mansfield can be an ideal spot to cast a fly to tarpon. Sometimes they roll on the surface down the inside of the jetty, on the channel side. In 1991, I caught and released a tarpon estimated at about 12 pounds from the rocks using a 9-weight rod. I use floating lines, variations of Deceiver streamer patterns, and a shock tippet for this type of fly fishing.

Wade Duncan, Harlingen

Standing alone in a silvery-gray dawn, casting to the rolling swells at the end of Port Aransas's north jetty, is a feast for the senses. The surf roars and vibrates through angular openings in the rocks. Warm sea water and foam wash across your ankles. Gulls cry out overhead in perpetual anticipation. As you stand on a block of pink granite at the water's edge, your first casts are almost reflexive—loop after loop of fly line thrown into the frothy troughs between rolling combers. That's usually when the first strike comes. There's a jolt, your rod bows up, and you stand wide-eyed as the fish makes a searing run. Your first thought is that this one is out of control, unmanageable, possibly unstoppable. But the second run is shorter, and you begin to take charge, steering the flashy shape toward the nearest flat rock. As the wave washes the fish onto its side, you see the gold spots on silver and blue and the angry eye and toothy jaw of a Spanish mackerel.

Within a 30-foot cast from seven pairs of major jetties and a host of breakwaters and groins along the Texas coast is some of the most accessible and underutilized saltwater fly fishing in the country. On some days, fly fishing from the jetties can be as simple as casting for sunfish on a tranquil farm pond. When the voracious little bluefish fill the surf, when wild-eyed ladyfish are crashing baitfish and Spanish mackerel are cruising close to the rocks, the fly fishing action can be fast and easy. On other occasions, stiff winds, ferocious currents, and blowing surf test the skills and tackle of the most experienced flycaster.

Although the primary purpose of these rocky appendages is to direct the flows of tidal currents and keep the passes open to navigation, Texas jetties have been a popular and readily accessible angling destination for a century. According to the U.S. Army Corps of Engineers, the oldest jetties at a major Texas pass are those at Galveston Harbor, which were completed in 1897. Few places on the coast provide as accessible a place to fish for such a wide variety of saltwater species as do jetties. The rocks concentrate forage fish that draw every variety of predator. From sharks to sheepshead, virtually every inshore Gulf species as well as bluewater residents like king mackerel and cobia, has been caught from the jetty rocks at one time or another. The shallow surf at the base of the jetties is a productive area for red drum and seatrout, and the supporting structures on the channel side of some jetties attract larger predators. The major jetties range in length from 2,300 feet at Port Mansfield to 35,603 feet at Bolivar Roads in Galveston Bay.

TACKLE AND TECHNIQUES

To be successful, flycasters need only copy methods that anglers with conventional tackle have used off the jetties for years. Look for frantic baitfish and bird activity that indicates fish feeding near the surface. The successful jetty flyfisher will also learn to identify favorable wind, current, and water quality. Like anglers with conventional tackle, flyfishers can benefit greatly from a knowledge of underwater structure around many Texas jetties. Deeper holes and submerged rocks rearranged by hurricanes are prime targets for the most successful jetty anglers.

Jetty fly-fishing tackle for most saltwater species is neither complicated nor expensive. An 8- or 9-weight fly rod mounted with a single-action, exposed-rim reel, counterbalanced handle, and 150 yards of 20-pound-test dacron backing usually is adequate. Most smaller jetty species can be subdued easily by palming a reel's exposed rim control feature. A reel with a smooth-running disc-drag system is the right choice for larger species such as big redfish, king mackerel, jack crevalle, or tarpon. On days when the cobalt blue water offshore has moved inshore, bringing larger fish like tarpon, king mackerel, and jack crevalle to the jetties, it is wise to move up a step or two in rod weight and reel capacity.

Having a selection of specialized lines for fishing around the jetties can help solve the puzzles and get your flies down to the variety of game-fish that feed around the jetty rocks. Although floating lines perform adequately in the shallow surf and over surface-feeding fish off the jetties, a variety of intermediate, full-sink, and shooting-taper lines can greatly expand the opportunities. An effective technique when walking the jetties or fishing the edges of the rocks from a boat with sinking lines is to rig a short (3-foot) leader with 12-pound to 15-pound monofilament tied directly to the fly. The short leader is important when using fast-sinking lines because it keeps the fly line in direct contact with the fly at greater depths.

The 8-pound and 10-pound tippets work well on the flats, but it is advisable to use a heavier leader around the rocks, where the larger redfish and seatrout hang out. Some anglers also select a 1-foot-long section of 20-pound test or heavier monofilament to serve as a "shock tippet," especially when there are members of the mackerel family about. Sometimes you can get more strikes from Spanish mackerel with a lighter leader, even though there is the occasional cutoff. If tarpon are your targets around the rocks, a 1-foot-long shock tippet of 50-pound test or heavier is essential. For king mackerel, a short (5- or 6-inch) section of wire between the fly and the class tippet is an essential part of the leader system.

In the fall, when cold fronts begin their annual pilgrimage along the coast and water temperatures drop to the mid-60s, flyfishers using specialized fly lines—including uniform-density sinking lines that cast smoothly, sink rapidly, and allow solid hookups at depths of 15 feet and more—can swim streamers and bendback flies through the "secret holes" that were once the sole domain of the jetty pros with their popping rods, plastic worms, and shrimp tails. However, because of restricted mobility while standing on jetty rocks, an extended fight with a large tarpon is problematic. Flyfishers will want to be well prepared for heart-stopping action. The uniform-density lines like 3M Scientific Anglers' Uniform Sink tapers go beyond merely dragging a fly down to a desired depth. In addition to providing better contact with the fly and more confident depth control, these uniform-density lines cast more "normally" than other sinking lines. You can feel the line in the air, control over your loop is excellent, and you don't have the sensation of merely slinging a lot of weight at a target.

An effective technique suggested by Galveston fly-fishing guide Chris Phillips for taking redfish and trout in holes along the jetties is to use a sinking line with a heavily hackled or spun deer-hair fly, such as a Dahlberg Diver or a finger mullet pattern. These flies float and at the end of a sinking line and a 3 1/2-foot to 4-foot leader, will bob up and down in the jetty rocks, attracting predators. When you strip the line, this fly will go down almost into the rocks, stop, and then float back up. It will not go to the top because it is in deep water. But it is going to drift straight up right off the rocks. Redfish and trout hang around in these holes along the Texas jetties, and if you can run your fly down and back up, invariably they will hit it.

JETTY FLY PATTERNS

Classic minnow patterns such as the Lefty's Deceiver and bend-back streamers, tied so that the hook-point rides up, are excellent producers around granite rocks and crevices and are less likely to snag. Any combination of white, red, and yellow bucktail works well. The Clouser Deep Minnow fly, a glass minnow pattern weighted with lead eyes, is another deadly profile in the rocks. A Clouser Deep Minnow tied on a 2 to 2/0 stainless steel hook with chartreuse bucktail on the upper and lower wings and a few strands of rainbow Krystal Flash in the middle also will draw lots of attention from seatrout, redfish, small grouper, ladyfish, and other jetty cruisers. Clousers tied with white or yellow bucktail seem to be the color of preference for Spanish mackerel. Yellow-and-red Clousers are effective on trout and redfish. Deceivers, Whistlers, and other glass minnow patterns also work well around the rocks and crevices of the Texas jetties. Be prepared to lose a fly or two when teasing fish around the rocks. The reward for getting a fly down into the right hole in front of a jetty will outweigh the loss of a few flies.

HAZARDS AND PRECAUTIONS

Anglers have been fishing off jetties for years, but some jetties are more accommodating to walkers than others, and some should be approached only by boat. When fishing off a Texas jetty, take care in moving about. Surfaces can be extremely slippery, especially when they are dampened by wave action and coated with algae. Most experienced jetty anglers learn to spot the hazardous areas and are careful where they step. With practice, it is not difficult to find a suitable rock platform where you can position yourself to cast a fly. After assessing the surf conditions, find a rock as close to the water's edge as possible. Surf and wave action and cracks and crevices in the rocks can play havoc with line stripped at the feet of the flycaster. Developing a knack for finding the right flat surface to perch on and judging the wave action can reduce these problems significantly. Wearing a commercially made stripping basket (or one made by putting two slits in a small plastic wastebasket and looping a belt through it) also can solve the line storage problem.

POPULAR JETTY FLY-FISHING SITES

Sabine Pass

The Sabine Pass jetties are located at the mouth of Sabine Pass on the Texas-Louisiana border. Like other Texas jetties, Sabine's attract a varied lineup of coastal species from trout, reds, and flounder to Spanish mackerel, tarpon, and kings. But unlike other Texas jetties, those at Sabine Pass are usually free from crowds, a bonus for flyfishers during the peak summer fishing months.

To get to the Sabine jetties, take I-10 to Winnie and Texas 73 from there to Port Arthur. Then head south on Texas 87 to Sabine Pass.

Separated from shore by salt marshes, the Sabine jetties are accessible only by boat. Boaters can launch from a county-maintained public ramp in the town of Sabine Pass or from the Texas Parks and Wildlife ramp at the Sabine Pass Battleground State Historical Park.

Bolivar Roads Pass

The north jetty at Bolivar Roads Pass, near Galveston, attracts a variety of gamefish. During the summer months work the edges of the rocks for trout, reds, and sheepshead and look for schools of jacks, ladyfish, bluefish, and Spanish mackerel busting bait on the surface. Walk-in anglers have 2 miles of jetty to prospect from the bait camp entry point to the Small Boat Cut. The cut offers moving water and attractive fish-holding features, but it can get crowded with boaters and is best avoided on summer weekends. The Gulf side offers protection from south, southwest, and west winds, and the channel side is protected from north winds. Flyfishers in boats have the choice of fishing another 4.3 miles of the jetty extending beyond the small boat cut into the Gulf.

During the summer, diving birds are a tip-off that schools of jacks and Spanish mackerel are herding bait near the rocks. Tarpon also are present from June through October.

The north jetty is located about 3 miles from the ferry landing on the Bolivar Peninsula, east of the lighthouse and Texas 87. Two miles beyond the lighthouse on Texas 87, take the road to the right.

Galveston Island

The north, or channel side of the south jetty at Galveston is protected against strong south winds, and the Gulf side, or south side, offers flyfishers a buffer from north winds. The Gulfside surf along the edge of the jetty and extending down the swimmers' beach is known to attract large jack crevalle, redfish, blacktip shark, and tarpon during the summer months when menhaden schools fill the beachfront.

The south jetty is located in R. A. Apffel Park at the end of Seawall Boulevard in Galveston. There is a fee for entering the park.

Surfside and Quintana
The Surfside and Quintana jetties near Freeport offer an ideal platform for flycasters working both the surf and channel side of the rocks. During the summer months, when clear, green water moves in to the beach on southeast winds of 10 knots or less, look for Spanish mackerel action from about the midway point on the jetty out to the end. Schooling trout, bluefish, Spanish mackerel, and ladyfish frequently gang up in the shallow surf, where they are willing targets for Deceiver or Clouser Deep Minnow flies dressed in white, yellow, or chartreuse bucktail.

With its flat surface, Surfside is one of the most accommodating jetties for flyfishing on the coast. Flycasters do need to be aware of the wooden rail that runs along the top of the jetty on the channel side. It is easily avoided when casting on the surf side by angling the backcast at a slightly upward angle or inverting the reel and executing a steeple cast. For peak action at the Surfside jetty, arrive at dawn. Spanish mackerel schools give their presence away with surface attacks on baitfish schools. Later in the morning, the trout, the bluefish, and the ladyfish often gang up in the nearshore surf.

To get to the Surfside jetty from Houston, take Texas 288 to Clute then Texas 332 to Surfside. After crossing the high bridge over the Intracoastal Waterway, turn right at Fort Velasco Boulevard and proceed to Thirteenth Street. A left at Thirteenth Street leads to the beach and jetty.

Matagorda Channel
The Matagorda channel jetties, located near Port O'Connor, are accessible only by boat. In recent years, flyfishers have successfully targeted tarpon around the ends of these jetties from midsummer through fall. Late evening is the prime time for tarpon. Anglers also can anchor up on the flats at the base of the jetties and walk out to fish off the rocks. As at other jetties along the coast, schools of jack crevalle, ladyfish, trout, and redfish often cruise within a short cast from the rocks.

The Matagorda channel jetties are located near the western terminus of the Matagorda Peninsula and are accessible from launch ramps and marinas at Port O'Connor.

Pass Cavallo, Port O'Connor
An ancestral tarpon grounds, Pass Cavallo continues to draw the silver king. From July to early November, tarpon in the 50- to 70-pound class often are found schooling and feeding on an outgoing tide in about 20 feet

of water and within 2 miles of the Gulf side of the pass. Large schools of ladyfish and Spanish mackerel frequently herd bait around the pass in the summer months, offering nonstop action for flyfishers with intermediate sink lines and shooting taper fly lines.

Aransas Pass (Port Aransas)

The north jetty on San Jose Island near Port Aransas is one of the most popular and productive angling features on the Texas coast. There are four stone and concrete spur dikes on the channel side of the jetty. Designed to support the main jetty like anchors, these rough, rocky structures with sloping sides also serve as gathering places for seatrout, redfish, and other marine predators waiting to ambush baitfish. Veteran Port Aransas guide Smokey Gaines advises flycasters to look for places around the rocks where the current eddies because of a curve in the jetty. This creates a natural gathering place for predator fish. He notes that the "jetty pros" with conventional tackle target these structures and depressions, as do veteran guides fishing the rocks from boats. In the spring months around these jetties, you often can spot pods of redfish milling around the edges of the rocks.

Most anglers turn right when they arrive at the north jetty shuttleboat pier and head toward the surf. But it also pays on some days to turn left and fish the rocks at the base of the jetty on the channel side. Trout weighing 3 pounds or more hang in holes around these rocks and can be taken on Clousers and Deceivers. During the summer months, ladyfish or "skipjack" usually are easy to spot around these jetties as they chase baitfish and attract the attention of diving birds. They can provide exciting action for flyrodders in the shallow surf at the base of the jetty and will readily take streamer patterns like the Lefty's Deceiver in almost any combination of white, yellow, red, and chartreuse bucktails. The north jetty can be reached via a shuttle boat that departs from Woody's Sports Center in Port Aransas.

The University of Texas Marine Science Institute Pier

Located at the base of the south jetty at Port Aransas, the pier itself is not open to the public for fishing, but its pilings and other underwater structures in the area attract a variety of gamefish including redfish, trout, and Spanish mackerel.

Fishing at night off the jetty rocks and pilings near the lighted pier can bring explosive strikes from speckled trout. Casting weighted lines that sink quickly in the strong currents and using streamer flies dressed on inverted hooks that make them virtually snagproof enable flyrodders to tease flies around these productive structures.

Casting into the turbulent surf from a jetty in Mustang Island State Park.

Mustang Island State Park Jetty

Located off Texas 361 between Port Aransas and Corpus Christi, Mustang Island State Park has two rock jetties on either side of a water-exchange pass that draw trout, redfish, Spanish mackerel, and ladyfish.

Mansfield Channel, Port Mansfield

The Mansfield jetties are reached most easily by boat from Port Mansfield launch ramps. Like those at other Texas jetties, the rock structures draw a variety of gamefish. During the summer and fall, schools of bull reds can be spotted within casting range, milling around the rock-strewn fingers that extend out from the base of Mansfield's north jetty. Also look for schools of jack crevalle in the 15-pound to 25-pound class blowing up on baitfish on the channel side. Anglers sometimes travel up the Padre Island beach in four-wheel-drive vehicles in hopes of finding tarpon and redfish feeding around Mansfield's south jetty at sunrise and sundown.

Fly-fishing guide Terry Neal says the jack crevalle start showing around the Port Mansfield jetties in May and June, followed by king mackerel in July. He recommends anchoring just off the rocks and chumming them up to within casting distance. "There is a lot of good fishing on both sides of the jetties," he says. "In the fall, you've got your redfish migrations, and you will have big schools come right up on the surface."

Brazos Santiago Pass

The jetties at Brazos Santiago Pass attract good shows of tarpon in the summer and early fall. Mostly juvenile fish in the 15- to 35-pound range, tarpon frequently can be found at early morning and late afternoon, rolling and chasing bait schools at the edge of the jetty rocks.

The tarpon action gets especially exciting at sundown, when schools of juvenile silver kings begin rolling on the surface or pounding away at bay anchovies herded up against the rocks. Using intermediate sinking lines on 10- or 11-weight outfits, work Blanton Whistler patterns in chartreuse, black, and orange; red and white; and orange and yellow along the edge of the rocks. Local flyfishers recommend a slow, smooth retrieve with foot-long strips, which allows the current to sweep the fly in front of feeding fish. Rolling fish frequently show on outgoing tides from the end of the jetty rocks to about 100 yards back into the channel. Experienced tarpon hands say it is best to resist the urge to sight cast to individual fish when tarpon are rolling around the rocks. The theory is that more tarpon are feeding down below, and swimming the fly at an intermediate depth makes a more natural offering to the fish.

South Padre fly-fishing guide Eric Glass says July through September is the best time to try for the small tarpon around the jetty rocks, with mature fish usually moving in around mid-October. Glass has caught many tarpon on fly, fishing from the rocks and from a boat drifting along the jetty's edge. "If you [stop fishing] before dark, you are making a mistake," he advises.

Glass says he prefers intermediate sink lines such as Scientific Angler's Monocore for tarpon and other species around the jetties. He doesn't like floating lines for jetty work because flies don't track as well behind them due to the turbulence. On the other hand, he says, fast-sinking lines can be overkill. "You can use them when the tide is really ripping, but day in and day out, slow sink is the ticket," he says. "Most of the strikes come at about 3 or 4 feet below the surface."

Other species caught around South Padre's jetties are ladyfish, mangrove snapper, trout, reds, and snook.

Anglers can fish the ends of the jetties in flats boats during periods when there are only light swells. Even then it takes some practice making casts into the rocks when the boat is pitching in the swells.

Drive-up fly fishing is also available from the north jetty on Brazos Santiago Pass. It is located on the southernmost end of South Padre Island, in Isla Blanca Park. There is a $3 fee for fishing in the park. Most anglers fish the south jetty from a boat after making the short run from area launch ramps. The south jetty can also be reached by vehicle from Brownsville.

CHAPTER NINE

FLY FISHING THE SURF

Angler's Log
Bolivar Peninsula Beachfront
July 1995

We came on a school of glass minnows that were being pounded by tarpon and sharks. All kinds of fish were in them. I made a cast with a white-and-chartreuse Deceiver . . . and there was literally an explosion. It turned out to be a 60-lb. blacktip shark.

I fought it and got it to the boat in about 15 minutes and I was proud of that. I asked my friend, who had never even seen a shark before, to gaff it. All we had was a short-handled gaff.

When he gaffed it, all I could see was water exploding, his elbow sticking up and a shark's head underneath it. The fish came off the gaff, still hooked, and the battle started all over again. I don't think I will do that anymore.

Ronnie Robison, Orange

Every fall, along the 367 miles of Texas beaches, flyfishers join other light tackle anglers taking part in a "sunrise celebration." That is what Corpus Christi guide and "land captain" Billy Sandifer calls the early morning feeding frenzy that erupts at dawn along the Gulf. The focal point for these fireworks are the migrations of menhaden, finger mullet, anchovies, and other forage fish that fill the nearshore surf, drawing reds, trout, ladyfish, and Spanish mackerel.

From McFadden Beach near Sabine Lake to the mouth of the Rio Grande below Brownsville, the Texas beachfront offers some of the most exciting, uncrowded fishing on the coast. Prolonged periods of light southeasterly winds that push clear water, or "green tides," all the way to the beach are the most favorable for fly fishing in the surf. On days like this, 35-inch-long "bull reds" will run the bars, and big speckled trout will be holding in ridges and pockets waiting to ambush finger mullet.

Billy Sandifer, a Padre Island beach guide who takes anglers on "down island" safaris in his Suburban, says he spends a lot of time inspecting the big schools of ladyfish that fill the surf in the fall. There are dozens of places with birds and surface activity to check out along the beachfront, Sandifer says. "I have gone out there and looked and in 4 feet of water seen tarpon and jackfish right in with the ladyfish."

Sandifer, who sports a tiger shark tattoo on his arm and a hammerhead on the back of his hand, has advice for flycasters on how to read the surf to find the prime places to throw Deceivers or Clousers. He suggests a drive down the beach, looking for pockets and dead-end guts—the carved-out ridges and holes that offer ambush points for larger predators. "What you do is watch the steady line of the surf breaking on the sandbar, and then all at once it won't be breaking, or all at once it will just run dead into the beach," he says. "You look up ahead of you 1/4 mile and you can see where it dead-ends right into the beach," Sandifer says. "When you find that, that is the old box canyon scenario, and the reds and the trout and everything else is in there." Subject to changing wind, tide, and current, these fish-attracting features require some beachfront savvy and a sharp eye to locate because they are constantly disappearing and reappearing along the 60 miles of undeveloped beach open to vehicle travel. Sandifer says he looks for periods when there is good water movement in the surf but he warns that the last two hours of an incoming or outgoing tide are virtually worthless for fishing.

TACKLE AND TECHNIQUES

When tossing a fly into breaking waves, experienced surf anglers recommend casting at an angle to the approaching waves rather than straight into them. Wave action will make it virtually impossible for you to maintain any line control and impart action to the fly when a wave is carrying your line and fly back to you. You will have better line control and better results by casting across the wave, and retrieving your fly while it is in the trough.

Under light wind and moderate surf conditions, you can scale down to 6-weight tackle for the ultimate in surf-run ladyfish action. A 2-pound ladyfish, or skipjack as they are called in Texas waters, can get into the backing, and a 22-inch redfish with an "attitude" will keep an angler occupied for a good spell on the lighter tackle. A favorite tackle combination in light wind situations in the surf is a 6-weight graphite rod matched with weight-forward, intermediate sink line.

Eight- to 10-weight outfits are the usual choice in the surf when flycasters must contend with extreme wind, tide, and current conditions. If a tarpon suddenly appears or you see large jack crevalle busting bait around you, it may be time to move up to the 10-weight rigged with a shock tippet.

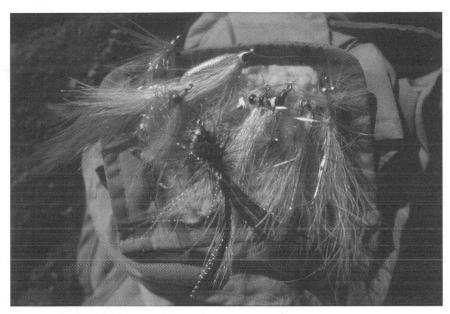

An assortment of saltwater flies.

Shooting heads, sink tips, and stripping baskets are good items to bring to the beach. A 9 1/2-foot rod can provide the extra leverage you need while being bounced around in the breakers, and uniform-density lines can be helpful in cutting through the swift current and getting your offering to the fish. With the fast-sinking lines, use a leader of 3 feet or less to keep the fly in contact with the end of the flyline.

South Padre guide Eric Glass likes to use intermediate density lines like Scientific Anglers' clear "Slime Line" or a floating line with a clear, intermediate sink tip.

FLIES FOR THE SURF

Flyfishers prospecting the Texas surf should always have a good supply of Clouser Deep Minnow flies dressed in white, yellow, and chartreuse bucktail. Glass minnow patterns and larger profile flies like Deceivers also produce well in the surf.

HAZARDS AND PRECAUTIONS

Currents and Rip Tides

Flyfishers have discovered how productive it can be to fish in the surf and around Gulf passes. But deep channels, irregular bottoms, and moving tides make these areas extremely deceptive and hazardous. A personal

Flyfishers in the surf must be wary of strong rip currents.

flotation device (PFD), or vest, may seem a bother for wading the shallow-est flats around these passes but it is a necessity for anyone unfamiliar with an area. It is also prudent for the coastal angler to recognize and respect the power of rip currents, or rip tides. These strong, narrow surface currents driven by the return flow of waves and wind-driven water flow laterally and then outward from a shoreline. They are most noticeable along the flat Texas coastline next to jetties and piers. Rip currents—another reason for anglers to wear PFDs when fishing the surf—usually diminish when they move into deeper water. Persons caught in rip currents should remain calm, stay afloat, and go with the flow. Avoid trying to swim straight back to shore against strong currents. Instead, swim parallel to the shore until free from the rip current. If the pull is too strong, ride the current beyond the breakers until it diminishes and then swim to shore.

POPULAR SURF-FISHING SITES

Galveston Island Beachfront

Fly-fishing guide Chris Phillips says some of the best fishing of the year comes in the summer months off Galveston Island. One of the places he targets are the rock groins along Seawall Boulevard. "They are fly-fishing friendly, and you have a lot of room for your backcast," he says. He recommends walking out and casting Deceiver and glass minnow patterns into the second gut for trout, mackerel, ladyfish, bluefish, pompano, and other species that frequent the surf during the summer months.

He says shrimp patterns also work well when used with sinking fly lines. "The current will carry them, and it is just like free shrimping," he says.

Pirates Beach to Jamaica Beach: West Galveston Beachfront

During the summer months on those days when winds moderate and green water moves in tight to the beach, the Galveston beachfront offers miles of explosive surf action. Flycasters wading the first and second guts have an opportunity to take trout, redfish, Spanish mackerel, bluefish, sand trout, black drum, and other species up and down the beachfront.

There are a number of public beach access roads along Galveston's Texas 3003 and Termini–San Luis Pass Road that open to miles of excellent beachfront surf fishing.

Start checking Gulfside beach conditions at Pirates Beach. Other public beach access points that lead to prime surf fishing include Galveston Island State Park, Jamaica Beach, Sea Isle, and Terramar Beach. On prime summer mornings, when the surf is laid down and green water has moved inshore, look for gulls and terns diving on baitfish or schools of mullet, bay anchovies, and menhaden that will attract predator species.

Galveston angler Layton Hobbs likes to wade the surf in the area around the Rusty Hook No. 1, a bait and tackle store on San Luis Pass Road at the Bay Harbor Subdivision. He looks for carved-out depressions and cuts along the surfline that could hold trout and other gamefish. "If you are standing on the deck of the Hook, looking up the coast, look to your right about 200 yards and you will see where the sandbar is cut in close to the beach," Hobbs says. "There is a natural cut through there, and on a decent surf with some good water, you can get the fish moving in close on those bars. On a northerly wind or a moderate southerly wind when you have just a little roll to the surf, or when the surf is flat, you will catch fish there in the mornings."

Fishing during the summer months, during periods when the surf is calm and clear, we have found that Clousers tied on #2 or smaller hooks frequently outperform larger Deceiver patterns. One summer morning, using a 6-weight rod and casting a white Clouser Deep Minnow pattern tied on a #2 hook, we took trout, black drum, ladyfish, Spanish mackerel, and small jacks in the surf near Jamaica Beach. Most of the action was along the first and second guts, within easy wading distance from shore. A feisty, 18-inch surf-run trout taking to the air in the early morning light leaves a lasting memory.

When the action cools in the surf, try different size fly patterns. One morning after casting a 2/0 Deceiver pattern and hitting a dry spell, a switch to a Clouser tied on a smaller, #2 hook drew action immediately, including a 22-inch trout that was shadowing a mullet school but preferred a relatively small glass minnow pattern.

Follets Island

Houston flyfisher Ken Brumbaugh frequently wades the Follets Island surf near San Luis Pass, near a sunken structure called the Car Bodies. Here, at dawn, he has taken Spanish mackerel, spotted seatrout, and sand trout. There are deep drop-offs in this area and it is advisable to wear a life jacket while wadefishing. Access roads to this stretch of beachfront are located just south of the bridge over San Luis Pass, on County Road 257 (the Bluewater Highway). To get to the Car Bodies section of beach, cross the Vacek Bridge to the Follets Island side. Proceed down the road just past Cold Pass Marina where there is an access road to the beach on the left. Turn there and proceed to the beach, then make another left and head up the beach, toward the pass. Travel until you come to a concrete bulkhead where you can see San Luis Pass in the distance. Around the second bar is the group of submerged cars. You can wade out and fish the first and second bars. Flyfishers also have had success taking trout and Spanish mackerel from kayaks on this side of the pass. With calm seas, you can anchor just short of the third gut, in about 7 feet of water.

Matagorda Island/Cedar Bayou Area

Neal Lillard, a former program manager for the Texas Nature Conservancy at the Wynne Ranch on Matagorda Island, is a long time observer of the air and water shows that take place on moving tides in the late summer and fall off the Texas barrier islands. "When the huge schools of fry are pushed to the surface by reds and trout, the avocets, cormorants, white and brown pelicans go into a feeding frenzy," he says. "The water is alive with activity." Excellent surf fishing is available at these times around Cedar Bayou, a fish pass that separates Matagorda and San Jose islands. The beachfront here is accessible by boat from the public launch ramp at Goose Island State Park, north of Rockport.

Mustang Island Beach

There are a number of drive-up access points for fly fishing the surf on Mustang Island at Port Aransas. Veteran middle coast flyfisher Jim Dailey says one of the best and the most overlooked places to fly fish the surf in the state starts in front of the condos on the Mustang Island beach. He says he picks days when there is low wave activity and the water is clear. "You can walk down the beach and look into those guts and see those alligator trout," he says, adding that it doesn't matter if there are hundreds of swimmers in the water. Mustang Island State Park, located on Texas 361 between Port Aransas and Corpus Christi, offers 5 1/2 miles of beach front for surf fishing, with picnic tables and shade shelters.

Padre Island (North End)

Padre Island is located about 20 miles from downtown Corpus Christi. The longest barrier island in the world, it is a low, barren, storm-swept strip of sand that extends 113 miles southward from Corpus Christi, almost to Mexico. It is broken only by the Mansfield Channel at Port Mansfield.

On this 60 mile stretch of beach, which is accessible by car, flyfishers will find summer and fall days when there is a modest surf breaking and clear green water tight to the beach the best time to visit. On such days, "bull" reds that are in the 35-inch class run the troughs between the bars, and big female trout cruise the washouts and dead-end guts (carved-out ridges and holes that offer ambush points for larger gamefish) waiting to ambush baitfish.

Padre Island National Seashore

Padre Island National Seashore is an 80-mile-long, virtually undeveloped segment of the barrier island that begins just below Corpus Christi. Visitors are allowed to travel by vehicle along the entire length of the Seashore, from the entrance near Corpus Christi southward to the Mansfield Channel, a manmade pass that bisects the barrier island. Four-wheel-drive vehicles are recommended for travel on all but the first 5 miles of the beach, due to soft sand and loose shell. To aid beach travel and rescue operations, large markers indicate cumulative mileage at 5-mile intervals. Park rangers recommend that all beach travelers carry shovels, jacks, and tow ropes or chains, in case they should get stuck.

Fall is an ideal time to plan a surf-fishing trek to the Seashore. Fishing is especially good a day or two after a mild, early season norther has calmed the prevailing southeasterly winds and knocked down the pounding surf.

Little Shell Beach

Little Shell Beach begins about 20 miles down the island and is so called because of the mass of broken clam shells that form the beachfront. Higher ridges and washouts at the water's edge serve as prime fish-holding structures along Little Shell. The section can be difficult to traverse without a four-wheel-drive vehicle because of the loose shell.

Perhaps because of its relative proximity to the visitor center at Malaquite Beach as well as its fish-holding features, Little Shell Beach is one of the most popular surf-fishing stops on all of Padre Island National Seashore. On prime days in the fall, flyfishers can find action with trout, redfish, ladyfish, pompano, jack crevalle, and Spanish mackerel all along this stretch of beach.

Big Shell Beach

Big Shell Beach commences below Little Shell, about 3 miles south of Yarborough Pass, and extends about 10 miles farther south. Big Shell is a favorite area for surf fishermen, especially in the late summer and fall.

At the 29-mile marker, beach travelers come to the Codo del Diablo, or Devil's Elbow, the name Spanish explorers gave this wind- and current-lashed stretch of the Gulf of Mexico because it is shaped like a man's arm bent at the elbow. This is where the Texas coast makes a left turn—a feature that means good things for surf anglers. The same devilish winds and currents that earned the area its name are still present today, creating the guts and bars that make the fishing so attractive when the winds moderate and the surf clears. Along this stretch, Clouser Deep Minnows and streamers will draw the immediate attention of trout, ladyfish, and jack crevalle, as well as pompano and palometa.

About 40 miles down the beach, flyfishers have the opportunity to cast around submerged structures, from big pieces of beached driftwood to rusted boilers from sunken ships. This is also where Sandifer grabs his binoculars to look for schools of tarpon beyond the breakers.

At mile marker 50, well out in the surf, travelers can see the smokestack of the *Nicaragua,* a Mexican steamer that ran aground during a storm in fall 1912. The wreck of the *Nicaragua* is about 10 miles north of the Mansfield channel. Here the beach begins to take on a different look, with dogleg turns and sharp ridges at the water's edge. At times, anglers can spot solitary redfish in the mid–20-inch class, cruising the clear, shallow guts a few feet from the beach. It's also the last stretch of beach near the Mansfield jetties. Here, Sandifer says, are a number of washouts patrolled by big trout.

A jack crevalle, one of the many species of fish that chase "rain minnows" and streamer flies along the Codo del Diablo.

Padre Island Beachfront: Port Mansfield to South Padre Island

In the late summer and fall, look for birds working over schools of ladyfish and Spanish mackerel in the clear surf right in front of condos in the South Padre Island resort area. Concentrations of "rain minnows" sometimes will draw predators right to the foot of the beach, and you will see gulls and terns moving up and down the beach to take part in these feeding frenzies. Six- and 7-weight rods are adequate, and it's important to have a good supply of Clouser Deep Minnow patterns dressed in white, yellow, or chartreuse bucktail.

South Padre fly-fishing guide Eric Glass has made as many as thirty trips a summer along the beach, looking for tarpon, redfish, and other species in the surf, from the resort area northward to the Mansfield channel. Although four-wheel drive is a must, an outgoing tide can provide favorable driving conditions on hard-packed sand near the water. "If you are down on that little apron near the water's edge, it is like a highway," Glass says. "You look for dark patches of baitfish, big masses in the surf that are scaled sardines or threadfin herrings. Then you stop and watch them." Glass says sometimes you will see the schools of baitfish around noon, when the light is very bright, and you won't see the tarpon rolling in them. But as the afternoon winds down, if there are any tarpon around, you will

135

see them rolling behind or among the baitfish. He adds: "The neatest single thing I have seen along the surf was one night at dusk. There was a group of tarpon that had pushed this one big school of sardines right up against the bank, and they were making these big, slashing arcs through these sardines within 2 feet of the sand." Another option on this stretch of Padre Island beach is to look for trout holding right up against the shore where the banks are steeper.

Del Mar Beach and Boca Chica Island Beach
These beaches are worth a trip for surf-fishing action. They are located on the back side of South Bay, near the south jetty at Brazos Santiago Pass. Pods of tarpon will occasionally show up here, but the surf is often off-color from the sediment deposited at the mouth of the Rio Grande.

South Padre Beachfront to the Mouth of the Rio Grande
Tarpon can be found up and down South Padre Island in the surf around pods of baitfish. Eric Glass says that sometimes he runs down the beach to fish around the mouth of the Rio Grande. The river mouth is an ancestral home for tarpon that still attracts these fish from time to time.

Occasionally guides will make a run down to the mouth of the Rio Grande to try for snook. Despite pressure from commercial fishing and pollution on the Mexican side, the river continues to serve as a nursery for snook, which need a brackish water habitat in the early stages of their life cycle. Texas Parks and Wildlife Department biologists have encountered increasing numbers of juvenile snook in net sampling surveys on the Rio Grande in recent years.

CHAPTER TEN

OFFSHORE FLY FISHING

Angler's Log
Production Platform Offshore from Freeport
July 1996

I stripped line from the reel and let it settle onto the cleared deck, checked the drag one last time, and made a few false casts. From the fly bridge, Capt. Mike Canino dropped Abra-Ca-Dabra's engines into neutral. Line snaked through the rod's guides, and the fly settled softly behind the idled boat.

It wasn't there long. The sensitive rod bucked in my palm as if someone had smacked it with a mallet. Lazy curves of fly line on the water sprang to attention, and coils on the deck sizzled through the guides. In seconds, the fish was deep into the backing.

At the 15-minute mark, I felt our team had the advantage. Played to exhaustion, the fish finally came alongside. It was a good king but not a record king.

Doug Pike, Houston (on landing a 11.5-pound
king mackerel on 6-pound tippet)

The 26-foot Robalo pulls up to an offshore buoy 20 miles off Port O'Connor's jetties and four flyfishers scramble to open hatches, dig out fly reels, and string up fly rods. ❧ The focus of their feverish activity is a school of small dolphins, or dorado, that have suddenly appeared right next to the boat. The golden green sides and neon blue-tipped pectoral fins of these offshore fish are radiant in the deep blue water. Everyone in the boat knows that any fly hitting the water will draw an immediate strike and a line-stripping run from these offshore gamefish.

It is early on a steamy August day, but it's Christmas morning for these flyfishers. Before the sun sets, they will fish a variety of offshore structures from anchored shrimp boats and tankers to buoys, weedlines, production

This angler casts to a weedline in the Gulf of Mexico.

platforms, and sunken wrecks. During the day, they will cast flies to ling and barracuda cruising in the shade of the shrimp boats and oil platforms and to tripletail and dolphin under matted sargassum weed. The little blue runners will bow up 10-weight fly rods as they power straight down into the depths after taking a fly near the surface.

A few pieces of chum thrown in the offshore current will attract trigger fish, spadefish, remora, and even the deep dwelling red snapper to within easy casting range. Hookless plugs teased at the deeper depths will occasionally draw king mackerel, amberjack, and bluefish into casting range.

Later in the day, closer to shore, there will be acre-wide schools of Spanish mackerel and bonito, or little tunny, to cast to as they thrash through bait schools under diving birds.

There are wonderful opportunities for offshore fly fishing out of all the major ports along the Texas coast. Many flyfishers who have honed their casting skills and timing on the shallow flats, sightcasting to redfish, are now being drawn offshore where they can broaden their saltwater fly-fishing experience and enjoy the thrill of hooking larger fish.

TACKLE AND TECHNIQUES

Experienced offshore guides don't approach an offshore platform or other structure until they have an angler on the bow with fly line stripped out, restacked, and ready to cast. That could be your best shot of the day. The

Oil and gas production platforms often reward
a well-cast line.

first stop could hold the best fish of the day, and you have to be ready when
you drive up. "It is a first-time deal," says Galveston guide Chris Phillips.
"The fish are not disturbed." He recommends if at all possible, motoring
around the structure so you can drift by it from up current so as not to
spook any fish holding around it. "Don't motor up to it," Phillips says.
"Use an electric trolling motor and come up to it quietly."

Boaters should also approach schooling fish with caution, Phillips says.
Running up too close to schools of little tunny will put them down, and
trolling motors won't keep up with them, he says. Instead, Phillips will shut
down the engine and drift in the area while chumming to bring the school
within casting range. Once the bonito are drawn to the boat, he recommends
a 7- or 8-weight rod with intermediate-sink fly lines to cast glass minnow flies
to them. He uses a 6-foot long leader and a 16-pound Hard Mason tippet.

For less demanding, non–record-breaking offshore adventures, Houston angler Doug Pike recommends a 9-weight rod and a tippet of at least

16 pounds. He suggests having at least a dozen fresh leaders at the ready as well as an ample supply of flies.

Port Mansfield guide Terry Neal recommends starting with a 10-weight rod. He notes that red snapper in the 10-pound class will power to the bottom after they take a fly, and it is important to have enough rod to stop them. "You will need something to lift that fish out with," Neal says, noting that the same rod will work on kingfish in the 15- to 50-pound class, which might turn up anytime offshore. He suggests a reel that will hold 250 to 300 yards of backing.

Neal recommends sinking fly lines and weighted flies that will descend quickly. He says his technique for snapper and king mackerel is to make his best cast and strip out some line, feed it back, and then strip it in. "A lot of the time, those fish are just waiting for some little baitfish in your chum line," he says. "If you are in 40 feet of water, you only need to get your line down 20 feet. These fish are suspended, and they will come up to take a fly."

Inspecting the Platforms

Flyfishers will encounter a variety of conditions as well as a variety of gamefish species around the many gas wells and platforms in offshore waters. Sometimes the current will be running so fast that it will be impossible to use chum effectively. In addition to prospecting around wells and platforms, look for floating weedlines, which attract dolphin and tripletail. Galveston fly-fishing guide Chris Phillips recommends throwing Clouser Deep Minnow patterns as close to the weedline as possible, then letting them sink to draw strikes from fish holding under the weeds.

OFFSHORE FLY PATTERNS

Red on white or green on white Deceivers with a streak of Flashabou or Krystal Flash tied on hook sizes from #2 to #3 are killer patterns for ling, king mackerel, amberjack, and jack crevalle found around offshore platforms, buoys, and anchored shrimp boats. Clouser Deep Minnows and other glass minnow style patterns on #2 hooks and smaller work well on school-size dorado and tripletail found along offshore weedlines.

JUMPING-OFF POINTS FOR OFFSHORE FLY FISHING

Upper Coast

Sabine Pass

Production platforms, anchored shrimp boats, and weedlines off Sabine Pass attract dorado, ling, tripletail, blackfin tuna, and barracuda. Veteran Houston flyfisher Frank Budd also has taken amberjack, blue runners, and red snapper on fly around production platforms 30 or 40 miles off Sabine Pass during the summer months. Budd says that many offshore captains locate fish around offshore structures by using GPS/Fish Finder electronics and then begin chumming. "At first you see the spadefish and the trigger fish, and a few minutes later you would see the reflections of the red snapper. They come right to the top, and you can pick a fish to cast to, in some cases."

Houston angler Shannon Tompkins, who frequently fishes the offshore waters off Sabine Pass, says ling start showing up off that area as early as March and hang around through August. The bigger ones come in early. There are numerous production platforms and pipe stands within 10 to 15 miles of the Sabine jetties. The buoys that mark shipping lanes also attract ling. From late spring through midsummer, Tompkins says, ling hang around almost every one of those buoys, and the line of buoys extends 25 miles. Ling are more prevalent in this area of the upper coast due to the many offshore structures available and the low level of recreational boating activity. Ling also seem to have a preference for offshore water in the relatively shallow 30- to 70-foot range, another feature of the Sabine Pass area.

Galveston

Within 20 miles of the Galveston beaches, you can find all the platforms and other structure you want for offshore fly fishing, says Capt. Chris Phillips, a Galveston fly-fishing guide who splits his time between flats and bluewater fishing. Phillips, who frequently fishes offshore on calm summer days out of a 24-foot center console, says he likes to explore gas wells, stand pipes, platforms, and other natural and manmade structures that draw ling, jack crevalle, dolphin, king mackerel, gray snapper, and Spanish mackerel. Phillips says some of the production platforms are within a 15-minute run offshore from the lighthouse at the end of the south jetty at Bolivar Roads Pass. Painted a bright yellow, many measure about 10 feet by 10 feet and extend out of the water about 20 feet.

On his way offshore, Phillips says he scans open water for schools of bonito feeding on the surface under diving terns and gulls. He says he has pulled up to platforms and immediately encountered large schools of bluefish. When this happens, an effective method is to work glass minnow patterns near the surface. "They will come up and bust them," he says. Tripletail is another species frequently found around offshore structures that will readily take a fly. Phillips says Clouser Deep Minnow patterns are effective on these deep-bodied fish with dark brown body and bright yellow dorsal fin.

Freeport

Fly fishing off upper coast rigs and platforms offers the opportunity to set IGFA line-class records. Fishing out of Freeport with Capt. Mike Canino on the Abra-Ca-Dabra, Houston angler and outdoor writer Doug Pike has come close to setting an IGFA line-class record for king mackerel on fly rod. In 1996 he attempted to top the existing 6-pound tippet IGFA record for king mackerel of 14 pounds, 6 ounces. His preparation included several hours at the workbench, tying Bimini Twists, Spider Hitches, and Palomar knots between leaders and the delicate tippet section. Hook points were sharpened and resharpened. Pike had two fly rods rigged and ready, one a 9-weight and the other an 8-weight. "Lines were dressed, drags were checked, and snake guides examined for nicks," he said.

Capt. Canino targeted an offshore platform that had held numbers of hefty kings, some exceeding 20 pounds. He idled the 46-foot Abra-Ca-Dabra to within easy casting distance of an offshore platform in clear, green water about 30 miles off Galveston. Sardine chunks were then chummed in the current, and in short order, the captain was pointing to a pack of "gray-backed predators making half a dozen boiling, gaping holes in the surface."

Pike's choice of fly patterns was an offshore baitfish imitation with a dark green back over an off-white body. The fly had a wide, vertical profile and closely resembled the sardines being used as chum. From the bridge, Canino dropped Abra-Ca-Dabra's engines into neutral—an IGFA requirement for an offshore fly-fishing record. The response from the feeding kings was immediate, Pike said, and the first run went well into the backing. After a fight of about 15 minutes, which required Canino to back down on the fish, the fish was at the boat. The scale on board read 11.5 pounds—a solid king caught on light tackle, but short of the 14 pounds, 6 ounces record for 6-pound tippet.

After rerigging with fresh leader, Pike had a number of other hookups, but all with the same result. "A few kings broke the delicate tippet with freight-train strikes and never gave us a chance," Pike recalls. "Others were halfway into the backing before their tails or dorsals cut the fragile line." After a series of breakoffs on the lighter tippet, Pike said he switched back to 20-pound tippet and landed several kings.

The excitement of fly fishing Texas offshore waters is unparalleled, Pike says. "Platforms off the Texas coast are loaded with big fish, and the pot sweetened when chum holds the players well within casting range."

Middle Coast

Port O'Connor

Mark Klotzman and his son, Spencer, offer bluewater fly fishing during the summer months for dolphin, king mackerel, blue runner, Spanish mackerel, bonito, and wahoo out of Port O'Connor. Klotzman fishes from a 26-foot Robalo, targeting a variety of gamefish around gas wells, production platforms, anchored shrimp boats and freighters, and weedlines between 20 and 40 miles off the Port O'Connor shore.

Port Aransas

Rockport fly-fishing guide Brad Smythe targets offshore platforms, gas wells, and anchorage buoys during his fly-fishing trips out of Port Aransas. He says July through mid-September is an ideal period for offshore fly fishing.

An excellent bluewater strategy out of Port Aransas is to head out toward the South Baker location, Smythe says, stopping along the way to fish production platforms. Weedlines that attract dolphin, tripletail, and other species often can be found in the vicinity of the South Baker feature, where there is often a rip current that attracts offshore gamefish. "If you find a rip, go down it and look for schooling fish like Spanish mackerel, blue runners, and bonito," Smythe says.

He says flyfishers also have the option of pulling up and fishing around anchored shrimp boats and oil platforms, which attract a wide variety of species. "Don't overlook the bite of a trigger fish," Smythe says. "They are aggressive, and a blast on fly."

Smythe prefers simple fly patterns with heavy lead eyes. "Bright chenille bodies with white bucktail wings and flash material are ideal around the platforms," he says, adding that he uses sinking lines, lets the fly fall, and then strips it back up.

Smythe says he has had the best luck with ling (cobia) from late summer into mid-September, when they are migrating through Texas waters and are aggressive in taking a fly. He says ling seem to prefer long streamer flies with hackle that swim and flow like Florida Keys–style tarpon flies.

In the summer months, when winds moderate and green water moves in close to the beach, anglers in center-console bay boats often can find ling, king mackerel, and jack crevalle holding around nearshore production platforms and floating sargassum grass. Small amberjack and blue runners will readily take flies around the production platforms. For king mackerel, use rods in the 10-weight range with reels with smooth drags that hold 200 yards or more of backing. When members of the mackerel family are about, add 5 or 6 inches of wire between tippet and fly.

Dolphin (dorado) are among the many larger gamefish attracted to weedlines and rip currents near offshore platforms.

Lower Coast

Port Mansfield

Terry Neal of Port Mansfield targets the string of subsurface rocks on reefs between 40 and 70 feet deep, which begins 13 miles from the Mansfield jetties. These offshore reefs, among the closest undersea structures on the coast, are ideal for fly fishing, Neal says. On days when bluewater has moved in close to shore, you can find grouper, tarpon, large snapper, and king mackerel holding on or near these rocks. "We can chum up kingfish in that shallow water, and you can catch snapper and sharks on the fly rod," Neal says.

Port Isabel/South Padre Island

Fly-fishing guide Eric Glass targets schools of bonito, jack crevalle, and dorado in the nearshore waters off the South Padre Island jetties.

SELECTED BIBLIOGRAPHY

Andrews, Jean. *Shells and Shores of Texas.* Austin: University of Texas Press, 1977.

Becker, A. C. *Redfish: How, When & Where.* Houston: Bozka Books, 1989.

———. *Speckled Trout: How, When & Where.* Houston: Bozka Books, 1988.

Bozka, Larry. *Saltwater Strategies: How, When and Where to Fish the Western Gulf Coast.* Houston: Texas Fish and Game Publishing Co., L.L.C., 1998.

Brown, Joseph E. *Padre Island: The National Seashore.* Tucson: Southwest Parks & Monuments Association, 1991.

Fotheringham, Nick, and Susan Brunenmeister. *Beachcomber's Guide to Gulf Coast Marine Life: Florida, Alabama, Mississippi, Louisiana & Texas.* Houston: Gulf Publishing Co., 1989.

Holt, Harold R. *A Birder's Guide to The Texas Coast.* Colorado Springs, CO: American Birding Association, 1993.

Jaworowski, Ed. *The Cast.* Harrisburg, PA: Stackpole Books, 1992.

Jones, Barry. *A Birder's Guide to Aransas National Wildlife Refuge.* Albuquerque: Southwest Natural and Cultural Heritage Association, 1992.

Kingston, Mike. *Texas Almanac and State Industrial Guide.* Dallas: Dallas Morning News, 1992–93.

Kreh, Lefty. *Saltwater Fly Patterns.* New York: Lyons & Burford, 1995.

Kreh, Lefty, and Mark Sosin. *Practical Fishing Knots.* Piscataway, NJ: Winchester Press, 1972.

Kuhlman, Chris. *Above & Beyond: The Original Aerial-Pictorial Guidebook to the Galveston Bay System.* Seabrook, TX: Above & Beyond, 1993.

Leavell, Lorraine. *The Original Guide to Family Fishing Holes.* Houston: Baylake Publications, 1991.

Little, Mickey. *Camper's Guide to Texas.* Houston: Gulf Publishing Co., 1996.

McAlister, Wayne H., and Martha K. McAlister. *Guidebook to the Aransas National Wildlife Refuge.* Victoria, TX: Mince Country Press, 1987.

———. *A Naturalist's Guide: Matagorda Island.* Austin: University of Texas Press, 1993.

Meason, George, and Greg Cubbison. *Pocket Guide to Speckled Trout and Redfish: South Texas Coast Edition.* Houston: Lone Star Books, 1990.

――――. *Pocket Guide to Speckled Trout and Redfish: Upper Texas Coast Edition.* Houston: Lone Star Books, 1990.

Richards, Carl. *Prey.* New York: Lyons & Burford, 1995.

Roberts, George V., Jr. *A Fly-Fisher's Guide to Saltwater Naturals and Their Imitation.* Camden, ME: Ragged Mountain Press (A Division of McGraw-Hill), 1994.

Stillwell, Hart. *Hunting and Fishing in Texas.* New York: Alfred A. Knopf, 1946.

Tinsley, Russell. *Fishing Texas: An Angler's Guide.* Fredericksburg, TX: Shearer Publishing, 1988.

Weise, Bonnie R., and William A. White. *Padre Island National Seashore: A Guide to the Geology, Natural Environments, and History of a Texas Barrier Island.* Austin: University of Texas Press, 1980.

INDEX